The

FIVE-ELEMENT
SOLUTION

Also by Jean Haner

Clear Home, Clear Heart:
Learn to Clear the Energy of People & Places

The Wisdom of Your Child's Face:
Discover Your Child's True Nature with Chinese Face Reading

The Wisdom of Your Face:
Change Your Life with Chinese Face Reading!

Your Hidden Symmetry:
How Your Birth Date Reveals the Plan for Your Life

All of the above are available at your local bookstore,
or may be ordered by visiting:

Hay House USA: www.hayhouse.com®
Hay House Australia: www.hayhouse.com.au
Hay House UK: www.hayhouse.co.uk
Hay House India: www.hayhouse.co.in

The

FIVE-ELEMENT
SOLUTION

DISCOVER THE SPIRITUAL SIDE OF
CHINESE MEDICINE TO RELEASE STRESS,
CLEAR ANXIETY, AND RECLAIM YOUR LIFE

JEAN HANER

HAY HOUSE, INC.
Carlsbad, California • New York City
London • Sydney • New Delhi

Published in the United States by: Hay House, Inc.: www.hayhouse.com®
• *Published in Australia by:* Hay House Australia Pty. Ltd.: www.hayhouse
.com.au • *Published in the United Kingdom by:* Hay House UK, Ltd.: www
.hayhouse.co.uk • *Published in India by:* Hay House Publishers India:
www.hayhouse.co.in

Cover design: The Book Designers • *Interior design:* Nick C. Welch
Interior illustrations: Jeff Dong

**Cataloging-in-Publication Data
is on file with the Library of Congress**

Tradepaper ISBN: 978-1-4019-5855-8
e-book ISBN: 978-1-4019-5960-9

11 10 9 8 7 6 5 4 3 2
1st edition, June 2020

Printed in the United States of America

This book is dedicated to Mother Nature,
the source of all healing

CONTENTS

PART III: FIVE-WEEK LIFE REBOOT!

PART IV: CHINESE MEDICINE FOR THE SPIRIT

When we try to pick out anything by itself,
we find it hitched to everything else in the universe.

—JOHN MUIR

INTRODUCTION

It was happening again, with yet another client. Lisa had her hand on the doorknob, ready to leave after a powerful session. Then she turned to me and, as if coming out of a trance, said, "But what do I *do*?"

The thing is, we'd just spent the last hour together, with me telling her *exactly* what to do! Using the techniques of Chinese face reading (an ancient branch of Chinese medicine), I'd uncovered her patterns of personality, explained how they showed us why she had the problems she struggled with, and gave her direct ways to solve them.

One of the most important things this age-old system revealed was that Lisa was a "bamboo" personality. The flexible trunk of the bamboo is one of its secrets to success: because it's able to sway in the wind, it doesn't get knocked down in a storm like trees with rigid trunks do. Like the bamboo, Lisa was a very flexible person. She could easily get along with lots of different types of people because she could adapt to their personalities, and that made her especially successful in her career as a teacher.

But every personal characteristic has two sides. On one, we'll find many natural strengths and benefits; however, there will be a downside as well. In this case, Lisa was "swaying" too much in terms of how she let other people influence her. Just like the bamboo bends in every breeze, Lisa would listen to one friend's opinion and be ready to act on it, but when someone else would voice another idea, Lisa would change her mind based on that new advice—until yet another person spoke up to say, "No, you should do this . . ." This pattern caused a "bamboo mind" as well, giving Lisa a terrible time with indecisiveness, procrastination, and self-doubt. Her thoughts would go back and forth, wavering about any choice, until she finally got so frustrated, she'd give up trying to decide at all and just put things on hold again.

These bamboo tendencies were the source of the problems Lisa was experiencing with her career decisions at that time. She'd become a teacher because both her parents had been, and they pushed her to go in the same direction. Even though she hadn't been interested in teaching, she let her parents' opinions influence her, too worried about their disapproval to not follow their lead. Now, seven years later, she wanted to leave teaching and choose a new career, to carve her own path in life. But her flexible nature was making it difficult to stand firm for her own needs in the face of her parents' opinions, plus the flip-flopping of her indecisive mind was making it impossible for her to figure out exactly what career to choose instead.

In our session, I explained how people with this bamboo pattern have a tendency to overthink things, and then to procrastinate so they can think some more, but still end up feeling so unsure, unable to settle on a decision. One key to moving forward was to understand that she *did* need more thinking time than other types of people. However, she also needed to learn to recognize the stage in the process where she'd narrowed her choices down enough. Even if she still felt unsure, there would be a point where she knew *enough* about each possibility to choose a direction. And of course, no matter which path she decided on, there would be some bumps in the road, because that's just how life works—it wouldn't be a sign she'd chosen wrong. In fact, she was actually much better equipped to deal with those problems because of her adaptable nature. While most people would only be able to come up with a plan B solution, she could think of plans C, D, and E as well!

I helped her understand why she was right that teaching wasn't the best fit for her personality, and we discussed several careers she was considering that would make her so much happier. I coached her in how to stand up for herself instead of letting other people too easily change her mind. I explained the timing of the steps she should take from here and taught her practical ways to not be so swayed by self-doubt and indecision so she could feel more confident about the plan she was forming for her future. Throughout the session, I saw her light up with big "Aha!" moments. More than once, she said, "That's totally me!" with pure relief.

And yet here we were, just minutes later, standing at the door, Lisa now equipped to move forward . . . and she was asking me what to *do*?

And this worried me because it wasn't an isolated incident. Some of my previous clients had said exactly the same thing to me at the end of their sessions, despite the fact that I'd given them so much direct information about how to deal with the problems they were experiencing. Up to this point, I'd review for them the most important parts of the reading they'd just had, and it seemed to help. Still, I had to pay attention to the fact that this kept happening. Was their new understanding fading just moments after they'd had these insights?

But worse still, when people returned for another session, I found I was giving many of them the same explanations all over again. While they'd often been able to use what they'd learned to solve the original problem they'd come to me with, they weren't recognizing that the new problem in their life was just version 2.0 of the exact same pattern. I knew I couldn't expect a complete breakthrough after just one session, but I felt I had to do something *more* to help them.

However, in that moment, standing at the door with Lisa, I didn't have time to review our session for her. Another client was on the way, so I quickly said, "What do you do? Here's your homework: For the next two weeks, take a walk in nature every day, wear more green, and go to sleep each night by 11 P.M. Then come see me again."

She looked delighted. "I can do that!"

I made those odd-sounding suggestions because according to the spiritual principles of Chinese medicine, these are some of the actions that can strengthen bamboo energy overall, and specifically create more ease in decision-making. I didn't think much more about my spontaneous advice, so imagine my surprise when, two weeks later to the day, Lisa walked into my office looking like a changed woman. While before she'd sat wringing her hands and twisting in the chair, she now sat bolt upright, brimming with enthusiasm. "I could hardly wait to come here today to tell you. I made my decision—I'm going back to school to be a massage therapist! After just a week of doing the homework you gave me, I woke up knowing what to do, and I feel more sure of this decision than any other I've made in my life." She went on to describe how her parents had tried to talk her out of it. "I felt my bamboo start to sway, but I caught it in time. I stood up for my decision and it felt great."

It suddenly dawned on me why people kept describing my work as "acupuncture for the spirit," and how that was truer than they knew. In assigning Lisa those specific actions to take, I'd given her something similar to an acupuncture treatment—not for her body, but for her life. What most people don't know is that when you go to an acupuncturist, their goal is not to heal you. Chinese medicine teaches that your body is very wise and knows how to heal itself *as long as its energy is in balance*. The goal of an acupuncturist, therefore, is to figure out which points to place the needles in your body so energetic balance returns; then they step back to let the wisdom of the body take over, and healing happens.

In that moment decades ago with Lisa, I realized in a flash that, in the same way, we can apply the *equivalent* of acupuncture needles—tiny changes you can make in your everyday life—to bring balance back and to heal on a whole-life scale. This is what I've been doing with people ever since, watching in awe as their lives changed as a result.

CONSCIOUS INSIGHTS AND UNCONSCIOUS SHIFTS

While conscious self-understanding is a powerful and a necessary source of transformation, it can be valuable to also have steps to take that work on an unconscious, energetic level to support that change. That's what happened for Lisa: she got new self-insight during our session, and the "homework" afterward acted to settle it further into her soul.

If you go to an acupuncturist, they will probably talk to you about lifestyle changes that will improve your health. But, of course, that's not all they do. They also give you an acupuncture treatment, placing needles in certain energy centers in your body to effect change in subtle but powerful ways.

And that is what this book will give you, based on my 30-plus years of study and research into the spiritual side of Chinese medicine, as well as my experience in doing thousands of personal consultations. I'll shed light on aspects of your personality and patterns and how to be more true to your authentic nature, which will give you insight into why you are the way you are. Then I'll guide you through "treatments" that can create solutions to the problems you're experiencing and bring you to a new place of balance so life just keeps getting better and better.

In Part I, we'll examine how this ancient body of knowledge reveals how each personality type has special strengths and natural talents, as well as predictable types of problems in life. You'll work with a questionnaire to find out which personality patterns are strongest in your nature, and what that means for your experience in the world.

In Part II, we'll discover how to choose remedies for the kinds of difficulties we humans struggle with, and then learn simple, practical little changes you can make in your everyday life that act as acupuncture needles to solve these problems, sometimes in seemingly mysterious ways. Although it may seem to work like magic, this is actually grounded in science, albeit a science that is very different than our Western one.

In Part III, we'll see how, if you're feeling totally stuck, you can do a full "reboot" to get your life moving in the right direction again.

Finally, in Part IV, we'll learn how to stay in the flow from here so any new problems that emerge are far more easily and quickly solved, and you can live in wellness, authenticity, and joy.

A NOTE ABOUT THE EXAMPLES IN THIS BOOK

I've included in this book many illustrative anecdotes from sessions I've done with clients. Though the substance of each example is true, I have changed people's names and other descriptive details to disguise their identities.

A NOTE ABOUT PRONOUNS

In this book, in order to avoid awkward "he/she" or "him/her" references, I've used the neutral pronoun "they." Interestingly, this was an accepted universal pronoun in the English language as early as the time of Chaucer, used for masculine and feminine, singular and plural. This fell out of favor during the 18th century, when the new rule was that "he" should be used for both men and women—and that certainly no longer fits for our times.

PART I

DISCOVER
THE MAP OF
YOUR INNER SPIRIT

*Most of your suffering comes from the lack of
understanding of yourself and others.*
—THÍCH NHÂT HANH

Chapter 1

THE FIVE ELEMENTS

Chinese medicine is a science, just like Western medicine is, but its approach is based on a nonlinear, integrative understanding of how the body works, rather than the linear, cause-and-effect approach we're so used to in the West. Chinese medicine was the original holistic medicine, recognizing the need to look at the totality of how the body functions as a whole, rather than just its parts. It evaluates relationships between the body's various systems and how they affect one another, for instance, rather than focusing on each single part as a separate stand-alone entity. Western medicine has tended to look at the body almost like a machine, where you'd fix a part to get it running again. Instead, Chinese medicine believes that no single aspect of the body can be understood without looking at its relationship to the whole complex process it's engaged in. And beyond simply looking at the body as a whole, this form of healing doesn't separate the body from the rest of the person. It considers the "bodymind"—how the psychological and spiritual dimensions of the human experience also are factors in our health.

This is not to discount the Western approach to medicine, which has brought us amazing ways to destroy disease-causing organisms, and medications and surgeries to cure life-threatening illnesses, for example, as well as many other wonderful developments in healing. However, its analytical, linear focus can make it miss the connections between things in any situation that are necessary in order to really understand what's going on, and to avoid causing other problems. Like looking through a telescope gives you detailed information about one tiny spot in the landscape but prevents you from seeing the whole territory, Western medicine can miss subtle but crucial information that is essential in order to bring true health and wellness.

But of course, Western medicine doesn't stand apart from the influence of Western culture, which conditions us to approach everything with the same mind-set. Research has found that in the West, we automatically tend to home in on the parts and not the whole, while people in Asia do the opposite—they look at the whole more than any single detail. In one experiment at the University of Michigan, for example, scientists showed a photograph to North American students of European descent and tracked their eye movements to see where they were looking and how long they focused on any particular thing in the picture. The students paid most attention to a single object in the foreground of the image. However, when Chinese students viewed the same photo, they spent more time studying the entire scene!

In fact, this difference extends to other Asian cultures as well. In a different experiment, Japanese and American students were asked to describe what they saw in a picture. The Japanese reported 60 percent more information on the background and twice as many observations about the relationship between background and foreground objects as the Americans did, while the Americans focused on a single item.

It's not that either approach is better or worse, but rather there are certain aspects of each that are valuable in our understanding of any situation, relationship, or problem. However, what I've specifically found is that our Western style of trying to solve problems is incredibly limited because we just focus on one aspect and try to "fix it," to find a solution without looking at the entire situation that may have caused or contributed to the difficulty. Whether it's trouble with health or a problem in life, we need to work with the unified system, including what's happening in our physical, emotional, psychological, and spiritual experience. This is why the linear approach to solving our problems that we've all been conditioned to use can be far too limited to be effective. We need to find more holistic ways to achieve solutions.

The good news is that we can benefit from the fact that, for over thousands of years, Chinese scientists researched and studied how to evaluate the whole in any problem, not just in terms of health, and developed what is actually an incredibly elegant and comprehensive map of how *everything* works. It's this map that master acupuncturists use to evaluate and treat your body, but we can use the same map to appraise and solve problems in all aspects of your life, such as career, relationship, self-understanding, etc.

I am not an acupuncturist, and therefore this book does not include specific treatment advice for health issues. All of my work is based on the little-known spiritual teachings of Chinese medicine, which I've studied for over 30 years, that are used to bring healing to your life—in other words, used to solve your problems (which of course can include positive change for your health as well).

THE MAP OF LIFE

It's time to learn the foundation of this system of knowledge that has been tested and proven over millennia, and to discover this map that shows how every aspect of life works. By now I've probably built up anticipation in your mind, haven't I? You're likely expecting that I'm about to introduce you to some vast and complex diagram that will take you years to learn to understand! But in fact, this map is deceptively simple, and initially, you may feel disappointed, or that this couldn't possibly mean anything helpful! Here's our look at the first version of this map:

The Map

Unbelievably simple, isn't it? However, in fact, it *does* take years of study to learn to really read and understand, but I've put in those years *for* you so I can teach it to you more easily in these pages!

THE FIVE-ELEMENT CYCLE

Here's how this circle came to be developed: In ancient times, Chinese scientists studied patterns in nature. They watched the movement of sunlight and shadows across the hills as the day progressed, and the characteristics of each season as it emerged and then evolved into the next phase throughout the year. They analyzed the life cycles of plants: tiny sprouts that grew upward toward the sun, blossoming, bearing fruit with seeds to start the next generation, and then declining, dying and returning to the soil. They observed the stages in life for humans and animals as well, from birth through childhood, prime of life, middle age, old age, and death.

What they came to see is that all of life moves in a circle, from birth through life to death and birth again. But within this circle, they noted patterns in how this passage plays out, a rhythm of five different stages in the cycle where the energy has distinct qualities. They called these phases the Five Elements and gave each a name to describe the kind of energy it represented: Water, Wood, Fire, Earth, and Metal. It's not that they thought life was actually made up of these substances; the names are descriptive terms to convey the qualities of each pattern.

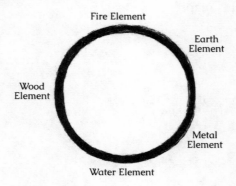

The Five-Element Cycle

Let's look at the meaning of each Element within the circle.

Water: Night, Winter, Death, and Pre-Birth

Water Element is the energy of night, when it's dark and silent, and we're sleeping, off in dreamland and not in touch with the realities of daytime life. It represents winter, when animals hibernate, and seeds hidden deep in the cold wet soil are soaking in rich nutrients and developing their strength. It's the mysterious land of the afterlife, but also of the time before birth, when the baby quietly grows as it floats in the amniotic fluid.

Water can be understood through observing its own nature too. What are the qualities of water? The ocean is deep, dark, and powerful, the waves relentlessly pounding the shore over and over, unstoppable. When a river encounters a boulder, it isn't blocked; it just flows around it. Water is an incredibly strong but at the same time effortless force. It just keeps going. The motion of Water is floating, yet it possesses enormous unseen potential.

Wood: Morning, Spring, Birth, and Childhood

Wood Element represents morning, when we've had a good night's sleep and can tackle the day with a fresh outlook, ready to dive in and get some work done. It's the vitality of spring, when all of nature bursts forth with new life. A tiny sprout has such a strong drive to be alive that it can break through concrete in its desire to find the sun. It's the baby pushing through the birth canal to be born, and the little child with endless go-go-go energy.

We can recognize Wood energy by observing actual trees as well. A tree grows up and up, its trunk rising in a vertical line. There is an active "push" to trees and all plants that is inherent in their design; it's how they're meant to behave. While Water has a floating motion and is about "being," here, Wood Element possesses a strong upward movement and is about "doing"—taking action.

Fire: Noon, Summer, and Prime of Life

Fire Element is the peak of the day, with the sun at its height and the heat most intense. At noon, we usually have a lot of balls in the air with several projects going at once. And Fire is summer, with all of nature in full bloom, and long hours of sunlight so even at the end of the day we can still have fun with backyard barbecues or parties at the beach. This is also the stage of life when we're fully grown—the time when we're excited to leave home and venture out on our own in the world.

Fire itself also teaches us about the characteristics of this Element. A glowing fire in the fireplace warms our hearts and lifts our spirits. The flickering flame never rests; it's always moving. The wildfire spreads across the countryside, looking for new things to burn. When people watch fireworks, their feelings are of fun, excitement, and exhilaration. The movement of Fire is outward in expansion and amplified speed.

Earth: Afternoon, Late Summer/Early Fall, and Middle Age

Earth Element carries the energy of the afternoon—a slower period when we're back at our desks after lunch with a full stomach, just wanting to sit and not have to work as hard as we did earlier in the day. Historically, this season was harvest time, when food was abundant, and we could rest after all our labor tending the crops. Earth also represents middle age, when we've had some accomplishments and aren't feeling as driven, and we want more time to enjoy our home, family, and friends.

Earth Element can be understood by literally looking at the earth as well. The ground is the solid foundation beneath our feet that provides a sense of stability. The soil is where the seeds are nourished, and the plants are well supported to grow to fruition. We say we are "grounded" when we feel centered and secure. Earth Element is a downward moving, settling energy and is about slowing down.

Metal: Early Evening, Late Fall, and Old Age

Metal Element is the end of the day, when we clear our desks and prepare to go home for the evening. It's late fall, when the trees lose their leaves and all of nature seems to be fading. And it's old age, when our own energy declines and we have to conserve our strength. In this phase, we're aware our life is coming to an end, and as we watch the sunset with our spouse or play with our grandchild, we may think, *This could be the last time*, and so we appreciate the preciousness of the moment.

We can also turn to nature to recognize the characteristics of this Element. Metal is represented by precious ore, such as gold and silver, which is highly sought after and valued in every culture. Metal also has to do with rocks and crystals, which are very dense, hard, and inflexible. In the natural world, the motion for Metal is inward, contracting and hardening, and then finally letting go.

THE FIVE ELEMENTS ARE EVERYWHERE

So the world revolves, each day goes by, the seasons pass, and our lives progress, all in a beautiful predictable pattern. We all know what to expect in terms of the phases of time in nature, but most of us don't realize that this cycle also applies to all aspects of our lives. This is the map of how everything works.

For example, it's the story of the creative process: you start day-dreaming ideas (Water); then take action with one of them (Wood); as you work, you experience the thrill of expressing your creativity (Fire); then, when you bring your project to completion, you feel a genuine sense of satisfaction (Earth); and lastly, you check for any final touches as you prepare to set it aside and move on to something else (Metal).

It's how cooking a meal unfolds: deep inside, a feeling begins to form (Water) and you realize you're hungry; you organize ingredients and get to work (Wood); then the action speeds up as you quickly mix and stir over the heat (Fire); the cooking is complete and you sit down to eat (Earth); and you finish cleaning your plate and push away from the table (Metal).

And any staff meeting follows the map of the Five Elements: people flow into the room in a random fashion (Water); they get down to business with a structured agenda (Wood); there's rapid conversation and brainstorming (Fire); then, as a group, they settle on some conclusions (Earth); and they clarify their final notes and prepare to end the meeting (Metal).

You can even see the Elements in how sex works! The mysterious stranger staring at you from across the room stirs inside you a deep, magnetic attraction. (Seduction is Water.) The relationship develops to the point where you have sex. ("Doing it" is Wood.) Sex culminates in orgasm. (Fire is the exciting peak of any experience.) After sex, you lie together and cuddle for a while. (Earth is about staying connected.) And finally, you roll over and go to sleep! (Metal is about separating.)

The Five-Element Cycle is a map that can be applied to anything to show you if it's complete or what might be missing, or to arrange correct timing of a process. You can lay it over a business plan to check if anything's been left out so there's a greater chance of success. You can apply it to the floor plan of your home or office to see how the energy will affect how you feel there. You can even evaluate a team to see if every part of a project has been assigned correctly. This is because each Element represents a personality type as well. So if you can give each person in the team a task that's a match for their personal strengths, rather than something they're not naturally good at or interested in, it increases the chances that each aspect of the project will be done well and on time and support the success of everyone involved.

You can use this map to see how to navigate the personalities involved in any relationship, personal or professional, as well as your relationship with yourself. In fact, one of the most valuable reasons to learn about this system is to discover your personality type and to recognize how your Elemental patterns reveal not only your unique strengths but also why you have the problems you do—*and* how to remedy them!

THE FIVE ELEMENTS IN YOUR PERSONALITY

Before you can start using this system to solve problems, you need to learn how the Elements make up your unique inner design. In this way, you gain insights into *why* you've developed the problems you have, and so choose the right solutions.

We each have all of the Five Elements in our personalities but in different quantities. There are usually one or two Elements that are strongest in your nature, and there is always one of those that shows where you "start"—it's like a default setting on a computer. Your primary Elements reveal your particular strengths and talents, and are your secret to success in life. They also show distinct patterns of perception and behavior that can limit you, or send you off course at times, or create obstacles that block your progress. But the good news is that you can use the map of the Five Elements to find your way out these difficulties and get back on track.

So let's move on to discover which Elements are most powerful in your personality! In the following questionnaire, you'll probably relate to at least some of characteristics of each of the five types, and that's because you do have all the Elements in your makeup. But there will be one or two categories where your immediate response will often be "That's *me*!" We can then use this knowledge not only to help you understand and accept yourself, but to find ways to stay in balance so your life can progress with greater ease.

Chapter 2

TAKE THE SURVEY:
WHO ARE YOU?

Remember, there is no one right combination of the Elements. Some people's personalities are one Element very obviously, with minimal amounts of the rest, while others have two or three Elements influencing them the most. We each have our own personal recipe; that is how we were designed to be! Your unique blend of Elements reveals your personal strengths and natural talents, but it also shows why you tend to have the problems you struggle with. And we can use the guidance of this system, proven over thousands of years, to solve them.

Complete the questionnaire below to find out about your personal Five-Element patterns. Take your time with these questions; really give them some thought rather than dashing off your first impression. With some questions, you may need to read them more than once to make sure you're not making an assumption too quickly about what it's really describing. Then, as we continue in this book, I'll explain how to use your results to navigate life in a balanced way, and how to get back on course when you need to.

WATER ELEMENT

Answer "yes" or "no" to each of the following questions:

1. You love to stay up late at night and feel it's your most creative time.

2. You feel things more deeply than others do, but you rarely talk about your inner feelings.

3. You don't like brightly lit environments; you prefer table lamps or mood lighting.

4. You have an interest in developing your natural healing abilities.

5. You sometimes feel alone in the world, or very different from other people.

6. You can feel constrained if you have to watch the clock or have regimented work hours.

7. You've had lower back pain or a problem with one of your joints.

8. Sometimes you fear that if you fully opened to your psychic ability, you wouldn't be able to turn it off, or you'd find out things you didn't want to know.

9. You love to soak in the warmth of a bath or a hot tub.

10. You believe your brain just works differently than most people's, and there have been times you've felt misunderstood.

11. When you compare yourself to other people, you feel you have a deeper sense of the infinite, or a greater interest in the unseen world.

12. You tend to base your decisions on an inner knowing that you can't always explain rationally.

13. Sometimes when you're around people, you feel like you're on the outside looking in, not really part of the group.

14. You're curious about communicating with people who have passed over, or spirit guides on the other side.

15. When it comes to deciding whether to say something or not, you often conclude it's better to stay silent, or else not say *everything* you're thinking.

If you answered "yes":

Up to 5 times: You have Water in your nature, but it's not your primary Element.

6–10 times: A substantial part of who you are is Water.

11+ times: Water is a major aspect of your nature! But remember that you also have the other four Elements present in your personality as well, though possibly not as strong an influence as Water.

Let's continue to discover more!

WOOD ELEMENT

Answer "yes" or "no" to each of the following questions:

1. As soon as you finish one thing, you immediately think, *What's next?*

2. You have little patience for people who wallow in their emotions.

3. You feel best when you stay physically active, and you especially love exercising in nature.

4. You've had the experience of someone trying to block your progress or prevent you from reaching a goal.

5. In the past or present, you've tended to get headaches, or had a problem with your jaw.

6. You base your decisions on analysis and common sense, not the emotions of the moment.

7. You have a strong desire to make an impact in life, to make the world a better place.

8. You've noticed you're better than most people at seeing the cause of a problem and how to fix it.

9. Anxious people who nitpick and fuss about every tiny detail can make you frustrated.

10. You're a lifelong student, always looking for ways to learn and to develop yourself.

11. If someone can't prove their point with logic, you'll probably reject their argument.

12. You've had experiences where another person tried to cut you down.

13. You feel it's important to challenge yourself in life, to always be moving forward.

14. You're too hard on yourself, and you tend to be too upset by other people's judgment of you.

15. You believe no one can get ahead in life without an action plan. It's important to set goals and achieve them.

If you answered "yes":

Up to 5 times: You have Wood active in your nature, but it's not your primary element.

6–10 times: A substantial part of who you are is Wood.

11+ times: Wood is a major aspect of your nature! But remember that you also have the other four Elements present in your personality as well, though possibly not as strong an influence as Wood.

Let's see what else we can learn about you!

FIRE ELEMENT

Answer "yes" or "no" to each of the following questions:

1. It's not unusual for you to think of someone right before they call, text, or email you.

2. If someone in the room becomes emotional, you can't help it—your feelings start to overflow too.

3. You're interested in so many things, it's impossible to pick just one!

4. You often base a decision on a flash of inspiration rather than logical analysis.

5. You feel Life is full of miracles and wonder why others can't see that.

6. You've been told you're too emotional.

7. You sometimes feel like you have trouble paying attention to one thing for very long.

8. At times you feel overwhelmed by your love for the world.

9. You use a lot of exclamation points when you write people!!!

10. You can multitask to the point that you get scattered or have trouble finishing projects.

11. You easily cry at movies or even television commercials.

12. You're quite shy, although most people don't know that.

13. You're fascinated by the thought that we may actually be guided by angels.

14. You have a tendency to be nervous, or have even had an anxiety or panic attack.

15. You talk with your hands, waving them around when you speak, no matter what the subject.

If you answered "yes":

Up to 5 times: You have Fire active in your nature, but it's not your primary element.

6–10 times: A substantial part of who you are is Fire.

11+ times: Fire is a major aspect of your nature! But remember that you also have the other four Elements present in your personality as well, though possibly not as strong an influence as Fire.

Now, let's find out how much your personality is affected by the energy of Earth!

EARTH ELEMENT

Answer "yes" or "no" to each of the following questions:

1. Relationships are the most important things in your life.
2. You love to decorate for the holidays and enjoy all the foods associated with each special celebration.
3. You sometimes feel like you're always there when anyone else needs you, but when you need help or support, you don't get much.
4. The best things about travel are the new friends you make and the different foods you can try.
5. You wish you had more time just to sit and relax and read a good book.
6. You want to be of service to others in life, and you enjoy helping people.
7. You tend to worry a lot, and your worries can sometimes keep you from sleeping.
8. You've had problems with digestive health.
9. You want to have a real sense of community.
10. You sometimes go out of your way to help someone and then check on them later to see how they're doing.
11. You love to cook or share meals with friends. Eating by yourself can feel lonely.
12. You sometimes get loaded with so many responsibilities that you wear yourself out trying to get everything done.
13. If people argue, it can be very distressing for you. You just want everyone to get along in harmony.
14. You can too easily be driven by guilt, or have a hard time saying no when someone needs you, even if you're tired or too busy.
15. Exercise is not your favorite thing, but if you can do it with a friend, it's more enjoyable.

If you answered "yes":

Up to 5 times: You have Earth active in your nature, but it's not your primary element.

6–10 times: A big part of who you are is Earth.

11+ times: Earth is a major aspect of your nature! But remember that you also have the other four Elements present in your personality as well, though possibly not as strong an influence as Earth.

Now we can discover the rest of your personal recipe by seeing how much Metal Element is in your nature.

METAL ELEMENT

Answer "yes" or "no" to each of the following questions:

1. You crave alone time at the end of each day.
2. You're sensitive to the feel of fabrics on your skin or are bothered by scratchy labels on clothes.
3. You tend to notice details most other people completely miss, for instance, spotting a little typo, or noticing a picture hanging crooked on the wall.
4. Crowded stores or noisy parties can feel overwhelming for you.
5. You don't have a wide circle of friends but those you do have are truly authentic relationships.
6. You have allergies, or food or environmental sensitivities.
7. You care a lot about the quality of your work and often double- or triple-check it for mistakes.
8. You don't like having to make small talk with people.
9. You've experienced entering a room and then wanting to turn around and leave because it just didn't feel right—but you couldn't explain why.
10. You've been criticized by others as being too sensitive or too picky.
11. You tend to breathe too shallowly.
12. You notice you can feel uncomfortable if someone stands too close to you.

13. You plan things further in advance than other people do.

14. It can be physically painful for you to see or even hear about a person or animal suffering.

15. You believe you're probably more self-critical or perfectionistic than other people.

If you answered "yes":

Up to 5 times: You have Metal active in your nature, but it's not your primary element.

6–10 times: A big part of who you are is Metal.

11+ times: Metal is a major aspect of your nature! But remember that you also have the other four Elements present in your personality as well, though possibly not as strong an influence as Metal.

Now tally your totals for each of the Elements so we can discover which are most prominent in your nature, and, in the next chapter, what your results reveal!

Chapter 3

THE FIVE ELEMENTS OF YOUR PERSONALITY— REVEALED

So, how did it go? Did you find that certain descriptions were right on target for you, while others you couldn't really relate to? Or instead are you thinking, *I'm all of them!* If that's the case, there's nothing wrong. Many people find aspects of each of these qualities are a match for them, and that makes sense because, remember, we do have all Five Elements in our nature.

However, even if you feel you related to all the Elements, there's always one that's your primary one as your "default setting." For many people, that one Element is obviously identifiable, while the rest are relatively minor influences. For other people, there will be two or three that seem to be active in almost equal measure, and the other energies are less a part of who they are. However these patterns weave together for you, this is not a problem. It's your personal "blueprint," how you were meant to be designed, and your job in life is to learn how to express that design in the most positive ways. And that's what this book was created to help you do: to make your life work in a way that's a fit for you. (And if you'd like more information about your personality, see the Recommended Resources at the back of this book.)

Every Element has many messages about who you are and how you can navigate life with confidence, compassion, and joy. But there are some major themes running through each that can help you understand yourself and see how to solve any problems you encounter in life. So first, let's have a look at what your results have to say about you.

WATER ELEMENT PERSONALITY

If you got a high score in the Water category, it's likely that you prefer to "flow" through life rather than be confined to tightly scheduled, highly structured days. Water people crave freedom, to come and go as they please, and to do what feels right as the mood presents itself. Water doesn't move in straight lines, and neither do Water people!

If you're Water, you think and feel more deeply than other people do. You process life emotionally and intuitively rather than with a purely logical, left-brained approach. And due to this trait, you need time to think about things, to just "be" with your thoughts until you come to a conclusion that feels right. Because of your inner depth, you don't make snap decisions—the thoughts need time to trickle down.

Just like there's a magnitude of life and activity in the ocean that's not visible to our eyes, there's a lot going on under the surface with Water people. In the same way that winter and night are still and silent, Water people tend not to talk about what's going on deep inside. It will seem to them that the right decision in any situation is to stay silent, or at most, to say the fewest words possible. If you tend to write four-word replies to emails, you're probably a Water person!

The ocean waves endlessly pound the shore, which shows in Water types as a powerful tenacity to keep on going, to be able to endure difficult times by tapping into their deep reserves of inner strength. If you're Water, you have a healthy sense of determination, and at times even stubbornness, which can be incredibly useful in terms of finding your way or preventing others from trying to control you.

You're a creative thinker with an unusual approach to anything you do, and most likely a nonconformist, who doesn't care so much what other people think because you want to live life your way. Water people are innovators, and often the ones in the fields of science, medicine, business, or the arts, who bring brilliant new advances because their minds work so differently from others—they think outside of the box.

But one downside of this way of being is that Water people can feel very different from most other people. Many have repeated experiences of feeling misunderstood by others, or left out, even ostracized from a group. In relationships, they can carry a fear of being abandoned, or they may have had actual experiences of being abandoned in their past.

If you're Water, you will crave time for quiet solitude, to just "be," and getting it is like vitamins for you. But it's possible that when you're with other people, even friends and family, to some degree you will still feel all alone. When we recall that this is the Element that has to do with the phase before birth and after death, which is not involved with connecting with the world, we can better understand why Water people in subtle ways often feel "other than" and not part of things. All this can conspire to create insecurity, fear, or trust issues for the Water person because they feel so alone and so different from everyone else.

Since it's human nature to believe everyone else thinks like we do (or should!), a Water person can be suspicious that someone is withholding information or keeping secrets. This is because *they* tend to not say much or even to hide things, so they assume other people will do the same. There can be difficulties in relationships due to this way of being. First, their partner can be confused and frustrated that the Water person isn't telling them things they feel they need to know. Because Water types naturally tend toward silence, it often doesn't even occur to them to say something. Sometimes, the Water partner withholds information because they've got such a deep belief that they're going to be misunderstood anyway, so they feel it'd be useless to even try to communicate much. And then, because of these same issues around fear and trust, the Water person can be suspicious that their partner isn't telling *them* things, and a vicious cycle develops!

Water is about "being" and not "doing," and these types can be dreamers, floating along with their ideas but not taking action on them. It'll always be important for Water people to eventually do something with their dreams, to bring them into existence, just as the baby developing in utero eventually needs to be born. Part of that process for them is learning to overcome any preconceived belief that they'll be misunderstood or ostracized for what they're trying to do.

However, Water people have a lot to teach the rest of us! Our culture doesn't value the *being* power of Water, and that's a real problem. Instead we're taught to value *doing*: constantly busy working, chasing more money, or racing toward the next goal. When you ask someone what they do during their downtime, they'll probably laugh and say, "Downtime? What's *that*?" But it shouldn't be a mark of pride to always be busy. The Five Elements teach us that we need to balance time spent doing with time devoted to being: regular downtime for periods of deep replenishment. Most people in our culture don't even get enough sleep, whether due to tight schedules or insomnia (which is often caused or contributed to by our frantic pace and splintered attention). So the benefit of being a Water person is that you'll naturally feel drawn to taking downtime, creating a nice ebb and flow to your day.

Water is the energy that allows us to think and feel deeply, and to not be rushed or pressured by others, but to align with our own inner flow. It gifts us with infinite willpower so we're able to endure difficult times and emerge still strong. It provides the desire for the freedom to live life our way, and not be restricted by social norms. And it imbues us with an intuitive wisdom that we can tap into for guidance at any time if we're willing to be quiet and listen.

WOOD ELEMENT PERSONALITY

If you found you related to the Wood personality type, you likely value logic, practicality, and common sense in your approach to life. You want to stay organized so you can get a project done and go on to the next thing without frustration or delays. Wood people are enthusiastic, driven, and goal-oriented, with their eyes on the prize, always moving forward in life.

This Element produces a constant inner tension that creates a "push," like what plants do to sprout through the ground in the spring. This can be experienced with Wood personalities in various ways. For example, they tend to be very direct in conversation, but some other types of people can perceive that as being pushy or confrontational. Wood people also like having a good debate, but others can think they're just being argumentative! This can frustrate the Wood person, because in their mind, they were just trying to get their point across to the other person, and enjoy a back-and-forth discussion.

This is also why Wood people enjoy staying active, physically and mentally, as an outlet for that inner tension. There's such a strong drive in their system that most don't like to sit still for very long. They love to exercise, especially if it's outdoors; and they're always working on *something*—making household repairs, or playing computer games, or brainstorming ideas about a new business they want to start!

Wood people have creative minds, but unlike Water types who tend to be dreamers and may not easily act on their dreams, as a Wood person, you'll want to *do* something with your ideas to make them real in the world. Remember that Wood Element relates to birth, so Wood people want their creations to exist in a tangible way. However, sometimes their desire to get going results in impulsive decisions, where in their enthusiasm, they take action before they've thought things through well enough. Then they're not successful because some steps in their plan are missing. They can see where they want to go and get partway down the road, but haven't figured out how to get to the desired destination from there.

Just like spring is about new growth, if you're a Wood type, you'll be a lifelong student, always challenging yourself to learn and grow as a person, especially if you can learn a new skill that you can do something with, rather than just studying to accumulate knowledge. And because this Element is the energy of morning as well, when we tend to feel more optimistic and ready to go, Wood people are able to confidently take on new ventures, knowing they can learn what they need to along the way in order to succeed.

Plants break through the soil as they grow, and Wood people are the ones who create breakthroughs in old, outdated ways of being. You'll be more likely to challenge the status quo or question unnecessary rules, and you have an innate ability to see what's wrong with a system and figure out how to fix it. Wood people thrive on analyzing ways to make things run more efficiently, and they're the ones who will speak up if they see a problem, to make sure it gets solved. They're always driven to make the world a better place, to create positive change that will benefit us all.

Wood people do best if they feel in charge of their own destiny and have a sense of forward momentum in life. Most have a great desire to feel like a winner: to reach their goals and be successful. If we think about the natural world, a tree is meant to keep growing upward, and it's not natural for anything to prevent that growth. So a Wood person will easily become frustrated if they feel they're not making progress. Then they can become angry with themselves, getting lost in self-blame and being far too hard on themselves. But they'll be even more upset if they think someone else is putting obstacles in their way. If they're not selected for a promotion, for example, their reaction can be to feel like a loser, one of the worst experiences for a Wood type, but they can also assume that their boss intentionally blocked their progress, whether that was actually true or not. No one likes to go for a goal and not achieve it, but for a Wood person, these patterns can really trigger them to react in anger, or feel shame, or even fall into depression.

Wood people often carry an unconscious belief that they need to prove themselves to others, and can have a deep fear of being negatively judged by them. Sometimes they compare their progress to other people's, as if life is a competition. Their fear of judgment can even be so great that they lose their inherent sense of confidence and then don't try to aim for a goal, because if they try and *still* fail, everyone will see what a "loser" they are. And this pattern can also play out in their personal lives in other, very subtle ways. If their spouse reminds them to do a household chore, the Wood person's perception can be that implicit in that reminder is a belittling judgment: "You're such a loser, you can't even remember to take out the garbage." And then the Wood type might respond with anger that the situation doesn't warrant. When this pattern develops in a relationship, it can become a negative dynamic that can erode their bond.

But the gifts Wood Element offers are so important for all of us! This is the energy that challenges us to always learn and grow, to continue to improve ourselves throughout our lives. It gives us clarity of mind so we can make logical decisions and move forward to successfully achieve our goals. It provides the confidence to stand up for what's right, to fight injustice, and act as an agent of positive change; to make the world a better place.

FIRE ELEMENT PERSONALITY

If you scored high with Fire qualities, you're someone who's easily in touch with your feelings. You'll be naturally warm and affectionate with others, and you feel joy at any heart connection with another person, whether that's in a lifelong romance or just exchanging compliments with the checkout clerk at the grocery store. And unlike a Water person, whose emotions run deep and usually aren't spoken aloud, yours are close to the surface and it's important to you to be able to communicate them. Fire people are wonderfully expressive and responsive, openly sharing their thoughts and feelings.

But some Fire types' feelings can flare up too easily—they can react emotionally when stressed, or take things too personally, their feelings too easily hurt. When there's a problem, some Fire people get panicked and do what I call "catastrophizing"—getting more anxious and frantic than the situation requires, and that can cause them to make poor decisions. At the very least, it can be difficult or take longer for them to calm down even after the problem is resolved.

If you're Fire, you're a free spirit, with a great need for fun in life. You have a lighthearted energy, and because of this, people feel better the minute you walk in the room. However, it can be a real downer for Fire people to have to work with others who are too serious or have no sense of humor. They wish people would just lighten up, because as long as the work has to be done, it may as well be fun for everyone! Sometimes Fire types are misperceived as being unrealistically cheerful, but it's just their nature to always look on the positive side. Even when they're sad, they're never that way for long.

Like a flickering flame, Fire people think fast, learn fast, and usually talk quickly too. But their attention can "flicker" as well! This means they don't focus on any one thing for very long. After they've worked on a project for a while, suddenly something else will catch their attention—*Oh, that looks like fun!* and off they go. They actually do best if they can work in short spurts, or even have multiple workspaces they can switch among as they go through their day. Fire people tend to have a lot of balls in the air, which gives them the stimulation they need, but also guarantees they can have trouble completing those projects.

If you're Fire, your energy always comes from your heart, giving you a warm radiance and an innate ability to make people feel loved in any interaction you have with them. But there's a corresponding need for *you* to feel loved as well, and Fire people often struggle with a fear of rejection. Even though they have so much love to share, they're often quite shy, and this can prevent them from experiencing love and finding real heart connections. It can even hold them back professionally; for instance, not taking a chance in their career for fear they'll be rejected, an experience that's far more painful for a Fire type than other kinds of people.

As a Fire person, you are very open-hearted, which is a wonderful quality, but there's always a downside to each of our characteristics. Here, we can see that an open heart is also a vulnerable heart. In their desire to express love, Fire people can let people into their hearts too soon, before they know whether that person can be trusted in that way. This increases the possibility that they can have their heart broken or experience a betrayal of their trust. When that happens, it can take much longer for a Fire person to recover than it would another type, and in trying to heal, they can isolate themselves, afraid to let anyone into their hearts again. For Fire people, the first step in healing actually *is* to withdraw, but only for a short time. Healing is completed only when they rejoin the world and start to love again, if only in little ways at first.

Chinese medicine teaches us that our consciousness does not reside in our brain, but in our heart. Since Fire people have such open hearts, they have a more open consciousness as well, so they are naturally more aware of others' thoughts and feelings. If you're Fire, you probably have experienced knowing when someone was thinking of you, or you may have felt their text coming before it arrived. Because of this open consciousness, a Fire person can also be an "emotional empath," who feels the emotions of others. This can cause them to be buffeted by a variety of feelings, and not always be able to discern which are their own and which don't belong to them at all. Often just the awareness this can happen helps the Fire person learn to recognize when a feeling "isn't mine!"

A healthy emotional heart needs to know how to move easily from one end of its range to the other. First, it needs to feel the thrill and excitement of expressing love to another living being. For example, you may see a Fire person breathlessly exclaiming to a blossoming tree how gorgeous it is, or exuberantly throwing their arms around a new friend. But the second ability the heart needs to have is to settle from its excited state into a peaceful calm. Fire people can have trouble with this second step because their systems are wired to constantly seek stimulation. As a result, they can experience overstimulation, for example, feeling scattered, nervous, having anxiety attacks, attention disorders, and/or insomnia.

But, oh, the gifts Fire Element people offer are so important! They model for us how to live with joy, and notice the little miracles around us every day. They show us how to keep our hearts open, to express love to others, and to be able to receive love in return. We can look at fire in all its forms to know how to successfully integrate this Element into our lives, from the thrill of feeling love like a flame flaring up, to a peaceful heart, like the gently glowing embers in the fireplace.

EARTH ELEMENT PERSONALITY

If you related strongly to the Earth personality, your relationships are probably high on your priority list, if not the most important parts of your life. This is because Earth people need a sense of connection, and they tend to focus their attention on others far more than themselves. And if you're Earth, you're also a natural "giver": exceptionally kind, caring, and responsible, for whom family, friends, and community come first.

An archetypal image for Earth Element is the "mother," and it's one of the easiest ways to understand this personality type. Just as a proverbial mother puts the needs of her family ahead of her own, an Earth person's first thought will be *How can I help you?* We can understand why a mother would feel this way toward her children, but a problem for Earth people is that unconsciously, they can feel that sense of responsibility toward everyone in their lives, not just their children! If you're Earth, you have an inherently nurturing personality; you're a true-blue friend, and it will feel unnatural for you to not step up if someone needs support. Earth people can have a hard time saying no, or may be driven by guilt, so if someone asks for help, they'll feel compelled to do so even if they're exhausted after a long day and still have more of their own work to do. And just like a mother, they can worry too much, their thoughts constantly flooding out to the people they care about, or all the responsibilities they feel obligated to handle.

Of course, just as it makes a mother happy to care for her child, Earth people find enormous satisfaction in helping others! Earth *wants* to nurture, just as Water needs to dream, Wood is driven to act, and Fire has to spread love! The point for each Element is to manage those energies because they can too easily overdo them. Water shouldn't float endlessly without eventually going somewhere; Wood's desire to take action shouldn't go into overdrive with no time to rejuvenate; Fire shouldn't keep their hearts open without discernment about who can be trusted with their love. And here, Earth needs to be able to set boundaries, to limit just how much they give, as well as to allow themselves to be receptive to support from others in return.

Often, these types don't ask for help because they don't want to bother people. It's the unconscious "mother" belief that their role is to help others; and it wouldn't feel natural if they were the ones to get help. Other times, they feel that even if they did ask, the help wouldn't be done properly so they may as well just do it themselves. It's like a typical scenario where a mother asks her child to do a household chore and it's done carelessly. The mother has to do it all over again, and mutters to herself, "I should have done it myself in the first place." So this can turn into an expectation that can prevent them from making the effort to get help. Earth people often have subtle emotional tendencies to feel disappointed, unsatisfied, or unsupported in life, but the more they learn to balance their choices in giving and receiving, the less that will happen.

Mother naturally sacrifices her needs for those of the family, and it wouldn't occur to her to do it any other way. For instance, she doesn't cook a meal and simply sit down to eat. She brings the food to the table, calls everyone to come, and probably dashes back and forth to the kitchen several times even as they start to eat so she ends up being the last one to sit down and feed herself. Again, this is normal behavior for a mother with her family, but for an Earth person, this can be standard operating behavior in all aspects of their lives, creating the potential for problems. If you're Earth, you may make subtle little sacrifices each day that you don't even notice you're doing. For example, you didn't have time to stop for groceries or cook a decent dinner because you worked late, so you just pick up fast food or haphazardly snack on leftovers in the fridge. You'd never treat someone else that way! In order to stay in balance, Earth people need to work on mothering themselves as wonderfully as they mother everyone else in their lives.

The concept of "mother" goes hand in hand with "home" and "family," and these are things that Earth people value highly. For instance, more than any other type, an Earth person often has a wonderful knack for creating a comfortable, welcoming home, a place they can invite people to gather. They also have a strong need to feel a sense of belonging, to find community, and friends who feel like family to them. And because mother is the one who nourishes us, Earth people tend to pay more attention to food than the other Elemental personalities. For instance, Earth types are more likely than other people to finish one meal and immediately start thinking about what they'll eat at the next, or when they're stressed, they have more potential to reach for food, to be emotional eaters, and to crave feeling full. And if you have an Earth person in your life, when you visit them, they'll need to feed you!

Earth Element is the energy that imbues in our spirit a kind, generous, and compassionate attitude toward others, as well as for ourselves. It gives us a sense of belonging with people who feel like family to us, and to enjoy helping others, as well as be receptive to support in return. Earth empowers us to stay grounded and centered, devoted to our work, so that our dreams are nurtured to fruition, and we can end up being truly content with the abundance we've created in our lives.

METAL ELEMENT PERSONALITY

If you're a Metal Element person, you're highly conscientious, with a natural ability to focus on what's most important in any situation. This is because, while the archetypal image for Earth is "mother," for Metal, it's "father." If we imagine the proverbial father, we know he has a big job —it's up to him to keep a roof over the family's head and to prevent anything from interfering with their welfare. This is an enormous obligation, and therefore he can't get bogged down in useless details or wallow in his emotions; he has to stay in control and on top of things. So as a Metal person, you're constantly vigilant, as if you were the father, feeling accountable for getting everything right.

A nature image for Metal is the sky, or "Heaven," and in terms of personality, this means people of this type have "high" principles, and always want to do the right thing. This influence of the "sky" also makes them take an expansive view of things, as if they were looking down from above. If you're Metal, you'll always tend to look back, recalling little mistakes made even in the distant past, so they don't happen again. You'll look forward too, often further into the future that most people, to anticipate everything that must be done, as well as what could go wrong and how to prevent it. This approach means that all your work will be beautifully done, every detail attended to, but it also gives you a huge territory to scan, which can create a constant anxiety or frequent sense of overwhelm.

Chinese medicine describes Metal as our "connection with Heaven," and far more than other types, Metal people strive for a sense of the sacred in their life, and they tend to be the most humanitarian of all the types. They put great emphasis on finding their true purpose and doing meaningful work in the world. Yet they often set the bar too high for themselves, anguished that they still haven't found their calling, or they're not doing enough to fulfill it, when to anyone else, it's obvious they're well on their path. They're often quite particular in relationships as well, searching for people with whom they can have quality friendships, not just superficial connections. This can be seen even in everyday interactions. For instance, Metal people hate small talk and consider it a waste of their valuable time; they want meaningful conversations with others. People of this type usually have only a very small circle of authentic relationships at any one time in their lives, rather than a lot of casual connections, but that's really all they need.

And the father energy factors in here in other ways as well. Even Western psychology says one thing all children wish of their father is that he'll be proud of them. Metal people yearn to feel genuinely proud of themselves, and to feel respect from others, but here again, their expectations for themselves can be too high. One downside of these characteristics is that their need for high quality, to "get it right," can make them perfectionistic and self-critical, as well as overly sensitive to criticism from others. This can be such a strong influence that they can overanalyze, get too caught up in every tiny detail, or anxiously procrastinate because they believe there is only one correct way to do things and it's all up to them to figure it out. One motion for Metal is contracting, which can sometimes show in their personality as being too uptight, not able to relax into a place of trusting things will work out, or that their work will be good enough.

If you're Metal, you have an intuitive instinct that comes through physical sensations. For example, subtle feelings in your body will inform you when the person you're with is stressed, and then you'll just naturally adjust your behavior to make them more comfortable. This is why the Metal person is often described as the "perfect host," very gracious and charming, always putting others at ease.

But this sensitivity to how your body feels means you're also more physically affected by the energy around you; in other words, you're a physical empath. For example, if you're in a crowded store, you may feel overwhelmed and exhausted by the energy of all the people there. Or if you're conversing with someone who's depressed, you may start to experience a heaviness, feeling weighed down or tired, because you're sensing their depressed energy. If you see a person, animal, or any living being suffering, it may actually be physically painful for you, and for that reason, some Metal people even avoid watching the news because it can just be too much for their systems. The fact that their energy is so open to and affected by the external world is also why Metal people more often struggle with allergies or have food or environmental sensitivities.

And because Metal types can get stressed by having to cope with the cacophony of energy all around them, they often need alone time at the end of each day so they can recover. They also feel better if they have enough space of their own in the places they live and work, so they won't be in close quarters with other people's energy. Often they think something's wrong with them to have to control their environments in this way, but in fact it's because they're more highly aware of and affected by the subtle vibrations around them than any other type of person. Having time and space to yourself is essential if you're Metal!

The gift of Metal is to help us always live in accordance with our ideals, and to inspire others to achieve their best lives. It directs us toward living our personal truth and helps us create authentic relationships with others. It imbues us with a sense of purpose and a focus on doing meaningful work that enriches our spirit. Metal calls us to always search for ways to refine our work and ourselves so we can feel a genuine sense of pride in who we are becoming.

You now have a good feel for which Elements are strongest in your personal design and how they can inform your patterns of perception as well as your needs and choices in life in both beneficial and challenging ways. (If you'd like to learn even more about how to identify and understand the ways the Elements combine in your personality, you'll find more details in my books *The Wisdom of Your Face* and *Your Hidden Symmetry*.) Armed with this knowledge, we'll now move forward to discover ways to use the map of the Five Elements to solve your problems, break through blocks in your life, and bring balance back by helping you return to your natural flow!

PART II

SOLVING PROBLEMS USING THE FIVE ELEMENTS

We do not "come into" this world; we come out of it, as leaves from a tree. As the ocean "waves," the universe "peoples." Every individual is an expression of the whole realm of nature, a unique action of the total universe.

—ALAN WATTS

Chapter 4

HOW TO CHOOSE
A TREATMENT

If your energy is in balance, life will be working smoothly for you. Your personal Elemental cycle will be in continuous graceful movement, just like the days, the seasons, and the times of life effortlessly move from phase to phase. Water emerges and then transforms into Wood, Wood moves to become Fire, Fire morphs into Earth, Earth changes to Metal, and finally Metal shifts to become Water, and the cycle begins again, in the elegant rhythm of life.

But because of the nature of being human, we're usually not in perfect alignment with that flow. Life happens to us. Beginning in childhood and onward, we have wonderful and pleasurable experiences, of course, and these are easy to accept and integrate. But we also have difficult or painful experiences that we don't know how to cope with or recover from, and this will send at least one of our Elements into distress at the level of our spirit. Even at an early stage, it can create or contribute to a problem in your outer life, even though you won't be able to see the connection. If your energy isn't able to return to a more balanced state, this disharmony can gradually develop to affect all the Elements, at first only on a spirit level, but eventually creating imbalance in your emotional health too. This then translates into more pervasive, long-lasting difficulties in your life. And in the long run, it can even manifest physically as a health issue or illness.

We can turn to the concept of using the Five Elements to "cure" these issues. When you can identify which Element is in trouble, you can use one or more of these energies to bring it back to health, and thus solve the problem and often prevent it from reappearing.

The foundation of Chinese medicine is the understanding that things are always changing, and health (physical and emotional) is defined as the ability to adapt to this change. If your Elements are in their natural healthy motion, you'll have this adaptability to easily recover when you hit a bump in the road and get back on course. But for most people, because of accumulated stressful experiences in their past, one or more of these five energies is out of balance, so they've lost some of their ability to adapt. Then, instead of recovering after each difficult experience, imbalance builds on imbalance, and eventually the wheels fall off the cart—none of the Elements are functioning well, and the person experiences major difficulties in life, or has a significant health or emotional issue.

However, when you learn to recognize which Element is the source of the problem, you can know what small, subtle changes to make in your everyday life that will act like acupuncture needles, to redirect the flow of energy, thus solving the problem and often preventing it from reappearing. In order to know how to do this, we need to understand how each Element affects the others in special ways so you can choose a treatment. It's an important piece of the puzzle, helping you regain balance in any situation so your life can unfold with ease and grace.

THE FIVE-ELEMENT CYCLE: NOURISHING AND CONTROL

So far, we've been looking at that simple, elegant circle of life and each Element's place in it. But this is not a static circle! The energy is constantly moving, with the power of one Element transforming into another. The flow is in a clockwise fashion, starting with Water.

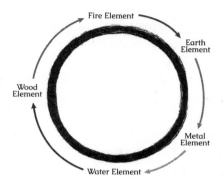

The Five-Element Nourishing Cycle

In the Five-Element Nourishing Cycle, each Element nourishes the one next to it: Water feeds Wood; Wood feeds Fire; Fire feeds Earth; Earth feeds Metal; Metal feeds Water. This makes total sense, of course, from what we know about the cycles of nature. The times of day: after night comes morning, then noon, then early afternoon, late afternoon, and night again. The flow of the seasons: first winter, then spring, summer, early fall, late fall, and winter again. The journey of any living being: pre-birth, birth and childhood, prime of life, middle age, old age, and death.

An easy way to remember which Element nourishes which is also aligned with how nature works: Water feeds Wood—trees need water to grow. Wood feeds Fire—you build a fire with wood. Fire feeds Earth—the ashes of the fire accumulate to form soil. Earth feeds Metal—the soil solidifies to form rocks. Metal feeds Water— the rocks create the supportive banks the river flows along.

The Nourishing Cycle already starts to give us ways to remedy what's wrong in your life. For example, if one of these five energies has gotten too weak, one choice would be to give a boost to the Element that nourishes it so it will then get revitalized. Or if you determine one of the five has gotten too strong and is in the driver's seat in your life too often, you can stimulate the Element it's supposed to nourish, which will draw the excess Element's attention and send some of its energy away in that healthy direction.

But there are other options available to us as well! Now we can look at a second way the Elements interact: the Five-Element Control Cycle. Just as each Element has the job of nourishing another in the circle, each also has the task of controlling a different one. The word "control" is not a negative one; it's not that one Element is trying to interfere or have inappropriate power over another. Instead, this is a positive influence, meant to help each of these energies grow, develop, and move in a healthy and measured way.

In this cycle, each Element has the job of controlling another one in the circle. Here's how it works: Water controls Fire; Wood controls Earth; Fire controls Metal; Earth controls Water; and Metal controls Wood.

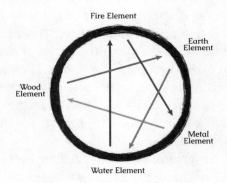

The Five-Element Control Cycle

An easy way to remember which Element controls which again simply relates to the natural world. Water puts out fire. Wood breaks up earth (as in the sprout breaking through the ground). Fire melts Metal. Earth soaks up water. Metal cuts wood (like an ax chopping a tree).

The Control Cycle now gives us new options for curing problems. For example, if Wood Element has become too strong, we might boost the energy of Metal, the one that controls Wood. In this way, as Metal increases in power, it's better able to reduce the excess Wood. Or we could choose to stimulate Earth, the Element Wood controls, to drain some of Wood's excess energy by giving it more of a job to do.

Now that you know the fundamentals of the Five-Element patterns as well as how the Elements move and relate to one another, you can use this knowledge to understand where a problem comes from and how to treat it.

HOW TO RECOGNIZE THE SOURCE OF YOUR PROBLEM

As you've seen, there's more than one choice available to you in bringing any Element back into balance. In fact, there are always five options, because each Element offers help in its own unique way. But how do you choose the best one for your situation? Here's where we have good news: There are Elemental clues in any problem you have that can lead you to the right solution.

But first we need to realize that in trying to fix a symptom, it's essential to avoid missing the *cause* of the symptom! The part of your life that's in greatest distress right now will be making the most noise and causing the most pain, so of course that'll seem to be the issue you need to focus on changing. However, if you only try to fix that problem and not what's creating it, the issue won't resolve. That particular symptom may disappear for a while, but new ones will now emerge from that same source—the place your energy originally went off course—that remains unresolved.

So first we need to discern where the issue originated: the root cause of the imbalance. And here's where we have some *more* good news! We actually have two ways to find that answer.

1. The Problem's Element: Any problem will have patterns in it that reveal the Element that relates to its cause and can show us the way to solve it.

2. Your Personal Elemental Patterns: Each personality type will develop a problem for a certain reason. So we can use our knowledge of your patterns to find out what's really going on and how to bring your whole system back into alignment.

Practice Session

Let's practice how we can find out which Element is the cause of a problem. For example, let's say you're dealing with exhaustion and nothing you've tried seems to bring your energy back. First, each Element offers a unique reason for ending up in this place in life, and now that we've learned about them, we have a way to recognize which one applies in this situation. Second, each Elemental personality type will have identifiable tendencies to develop a problem. So, knowing our personal patterns also helps us discover which is the cause of this imbalance.

1. Water Element: For any of us, this Element can end up in exhaustion despite its deep supply of willpower in our system—that inner strength that gives us the ability to push through difficult times. For example, having to endure a long-term problem without relief can result in exhaustion for anyone. Whether in one long difficult period or repeated times of adversity where there was no choice but to summon your strength each day and just keep going, you may have had to draw from your Water too often—and even the deepest well will eventually run dry. Or if someone went through a long illness and is now healed, their spirit can be deeply fatigued. If they had to power through on faith, not knowing whether they'd regain their health, that would also require them to keep summoning their Water energy to make it through, until it was nearly used up.

Water personality: If Water Element is a major part of your personality, on some level you'll be aware of your inner strength. As a result you may carry an unconscious belief that you *always* have to be strong. In that case, you may time and time again ignore your tiredness to work late at night, or put off your retirement, or even create or contribute to situations that require you to endure more than one human should have to. Sooner or later, even a robust Water type can lose power and become bone-tired.

2. Wood Element: Wood energy can take you to the point of exhaustion but for different reasons than Water. Remember Wood gives you drive, that focus on action, moving forward, and getting things done. And just like any Element, Wood's positive power can go into excess and cause real problems. For instance, have you been burning the candle at both ends, fighting tight deadlines while not getting enough sleep? Or are you caught in a fast-paced schedule where you have to dash from one place to the next, or finish one project but barely take a breath before starting on the next one? Huff, puff, those are all Wood Element situations! In times like these, it's inevitable that this energy is being called upon far too much, and eventually, the system crashes.

Wood personality: If you're a person with a lot of Wood energy, you naturally focus on "doing"—working hard to get ahead and reach your goals as fast as you can. That's one of your greatest powers but it has a downside: your Wood could develop a compulsive hyperfocus so you're "doing" *all* the time. This type of person may get up early to exercise before work, jam at their job all day long, then grab a quick dinner and head to the gym for yet another workout, or dive into focusing on the business they're growing on the side. And if this pace keeps up too long, they can hit the wall and experience deep fatigue.

3. Fire Element: This energy has risks for exhaustion that are very different from Water's or Wood's. One cause of Fire weariness can stem from the heart being thwarted in its desire to find love. For example, if you were in a serious long-term relationship that ended in heartbreak, or if you've been looking for love for a very long time, actively dating without any luck, your heart can feel so deeply tired. When you've searched for love so hard and for so long, and still nothing has worked, it can be deflating to your Fire. Or if you've experienced a significant betrayal, it can diminish this energy. This doesn't have to be in romance. For instance, if you discover a friend betrayed you by spreading gossip about you, or a business client cheated you, this can make you feel so hurt and unsafe, you may become emotionally burned out and unable to go on.

Fire personality: If you have a lot of Fire in your nature, you have even more potential to become emotionally exhausted for the reasons described above. But in addition, your tendency to constantly seek excitement and stimulation can get to be too much. Fire does need to have that kind of lifestyle, but within reason! If you have too much going on, your mind can get scattered and overstimulated; and your days will be spent running around like crazy, till at some point your system goes haywire and tips over into burnout.

4. Earth Element: This is the energy that gives you your sense of responsibility, but also creates the potential to be too easily influenced by it. This can prevent you from relaxing now and then in your day, pausing to take a break or enjoy yourself a little, because it'll nag you that there's still so much you have to get done before the day is over. Remember that this is "mother" energy, and one program Earth can run in your mind is similar to the old adage that "a woman's work is never done." And if you have taken on, or been given, too many responsibilities so there's no "me" time left, this can be an Earth cause of deep weariness. For example, if you need to care for an elderly parent on top of all your other obligations without enough support, this can tip you over the edge.

Earth personality: If you are Earth, your vitality can be drained even if you're not working so hard to care for others but are just *worrying* about everyone in your life. Energy follows thought, of course, and because Earth people's thoughts are constantly going out to others, over time, it can bring them to the point of feeling totally worn out. Alternatively, some people who have this pattern develop a heavy resentment because of all the demands others have made on them, and the weight of this feeling can also create long-lasting fatigue.

5. Metal Element: This type of energy makes us strive to always do our very best, to achieve something we can feel genuinely proud of. That can be quite a tall order, especially if you don't understand that it's usually only in the later stages of a project, or in life, when you've had experiences with trial and error that teach you how to do it better each time. So you may tire yourself out with overwork, trying to get things just right, or taking time to double- and triple-check details unnecessarily. And to one degree or another, for each of us, this Element carries the voice of that inner critic who says nothing you do is ever good enough. Every time it speaks, your energy tightens and contracts in response, and if this goes on too long, your poor system can get worn down to the point of both physical and emotional exhaustion.

Metal personality: If you're a Metal person, it's likely you're hypervigilant, unconsciously believing you have to stay on top of things every moment because if some little thing goes wrong, it could create a domino effect that affects everything else. This anxiety can take an enormous energetic toll on your system, to always be on high alert this way. It also could be that as a physical empath, your system is overwhelmed from constantly coping with all the energy of the people around you, and so eventually you end up deeply fatigued.

EVERYTHING IS INTERCONNECTED— YOU CAN'T DO THIS WRONG

The examples we've just discussed show ways to recognize the source of a problem, which then empowers you to find the right Elemental solution for it. In fact, there are always five options for bringing any Element back into balance, because each Element offers help in its own unique way. But you may be thinking, *Yikes, how in the world can I be sure to find the right one? What if I choose the wrong Element and make things worse?* Well, I have some very reassuring news for you: you can't do this wrong.

A colleague of mine is both a doctor and a Five-Element acupuncturist who trains other M.D.s in using the Five Elements to diagnose and develop a Western medical treatment plan for their patients. As part of their training, these doctors do case studies and submit them to him for review. My friend is frequently exasperated because, despite all his careful teaching, many of them choose the entirely wrong Element to treat—and yet, it still works! Why? Because eventually the energy will travel around the circle till it reaches the right one after all.

Remember how the circle is always moving, each Element transforming into the next one in the cycle? Let's say that you have a problem that should be given an Earth Element remedy to solve it; however, you mistakenly choose Water instead. Well, you've just made Water healthier, and as a result, it becomes a better source of nourishment for Wood. So now Wood is well fed and, as a result, gives a nice boost to Fire. And Fire is the Element that feeds Earth, so voila! Earth gets healed after all; it just takes longer than if you'd addressed it directly.

So relax: even if your choice isn't on target, you can't do any harm. Because the Elements are all interconnected, the energy will work its way through the cycle till it eventually reaches the Element that *does* need support, and balance will return.

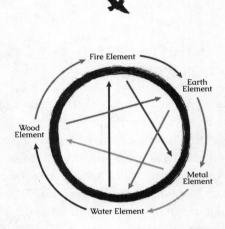

The Five-Element Nourishing and Control Cycles

The Five-Element map is a powerful guide to resolve things, not only when there's a single problem, but also when we're feeling lost, or broken, or stuck, or we just want life to work more smoothly. In the next chapters, we'll discover common symptoms of imbalances in each Element, how to apply a simple remedy treatment for a short-term difficulty, and how to use a full prescription for more pervasive issues.

Chapter 5

WATER ELEMENT AND SYMPTOMS OF WATER IMBALANCES— FEAR, LACK OF TRUST, LONELINESS, AND HEALTH ISSUES

Let's bring to mind what we know about Water: It's the first Element in the cycle and the last, representing both the initial glimmer of creation and also the phase after its end. It's winter, when the year begins and ends, and night, when we're deep asleep, resting in our unconscious world.

This is the time at the beginning of life, the energy of the baby floating in darkness in utero, not yet ready to be born, but it's also the infinite space that we pass into after death. Water is the unknown, mysterious place, not of this world, that we all emerge from and return to in the endless cycle of life.

This Element is also represented by Winter, when the world turns dark, cold, and still. It appears that nothing's growing, but in fact, life has gone underground, the seeds soaking in the rich nutrients from the cold, wet, fertile soil. It's because they're allowed a long time to develop in this way that when spring comes, each plant will have the power and strength to grow to its fullest potential.

49

And the energy of Water relates to the dark night, when we drift in dreamland, not in touch with reality but instead with our most hidden selves that live below the surface of our waking awareness. Sleep is when we process emotionally, and when intuitive messages can rise from below our normal consciousness.

We can look at water itself too, to understand its qualities: The stream flows freely in curves, not straight lines. The ocean's silent depths conceal a whole other world beneath the surface. Water can take the form of roaring waves endlessly crashing on the shore, yet water can also be a still, peaceful lake.

Chinese medicine teaches that Water is our deepest power, a rich soup of traits and talents inherited from our ancestors mixed with our individual creative abilities. It gives us a sense of independence and relieves us of the need for validation from others because we have the courage to go it alone. Water provides that inner strength that gives us the determination to push through difficult times; along with the intuitive wisdom we can tap into that lets us flow in life, trusting the process and not trying to push the river.

If you didn't resonate strongly with the Water personality type, this energy could be a blind spot for you because you'll naturally tend to disregard it in favor of the Elements that are more familiar to you. I often see problems stemming from Water in the lives of people whose main personality traits are another Element, simply because they're not inherently drawn to include Water-type choices in their lifestyle. For example, they can overwork and not take enough downtime for Watery rest and replenishment. Or they can be cut off from their intuition, like my left-brained client Madison, an attorney for whom it would have been a foreign experience to just relax into that more right-brain state of mind. Her highly analytical approach had shut down her intuitive side, and because she didn't listen to her instincts, she lost cases and missed career opportunities.

If you did recognize yourself as a Water person, then it's possible you *do* lead a Watery lifestyle, but in your case, the risk is that you can swing to the other end of the spectrum and overdo it. For instance, a Water person can struggle with fear, losing touch with the facts of their situation, and getting swept away imagining frightening scenarios. Jacob was treading water in life, unable to move forward to make his dreams a reality. At 30, he was still living with his parents, and though he was a trained musician, he didn't pursue many chances to perform. He'd heard so many horror stories about people withholding payments to musicians that he didn't trust club owners or even his fellow performers when they invited him to join their group. Instead of realistic analysis, he had an unreasonable suspicion of any offer that came his way.

No matter how much Water is a part of your true nature, if this Element goes out of balance in your life, problems can manifest. Let's look at three common issues that disharmonies in Water create, and then discover remedies for solving them, whether they're temporarily interfering with your life, or instead are ongoing, long-term struggles.

THREE COMMON SYMPTOMS OF WATER IMBALANCE

1. Fear

Each of the Five Elements has an emotion associated with it, and for Water, it's fear. Chinese medicine teaches us that fear has a rational side and an irrational one. Rational fear helps us assess risk; it reminds us to look both ways before we step off the curb so we don't get hit by a bus. Irrational fear would be if we don't get out of bed because we're afraid of being hit by a bus! It's not based on realistic thought.

This emotion is not the same as anxiety or worry. It's a deep, cold, often paralyzing feeling that freezes you in your tracks, as if water has turned to ice. When fear is creating a problem in your life, it's the irrational kind, without basis in reality. It makes you feel as if there is real danger that you might not survive, so the unconscious reaction is to stop and not move forward, because you'd just be heading into perilous waters.

If Water Is Not Your Strongest Element

Even if you don't relate much to Water, there can still be times when you feel blocked by fear, of course. If it's not dealt with, it can begin to impact the rest of your Elements, and therefore the entirety of your life. For example, if you're staying in a relationship because you don't think you can survive on your own, this could be due, in whole or in part, to a Water fear issue. Or if you're staying silent, hiding your feelings from a friend, afraid to say something that might be misunderstood, this can also be rooted in a Water imbalance. My client Patrick was so insecure that he kept secrets about himself from his new girlfriend because he was caught up in a distressing belief that she would leave if he revealed too much too soon. A fear of abandonment is an example of this Element's kind of problem.

If You Are a Water Element Type

If you're a Water person, fear can affect you in many different ways. You may feel a subtle but constant insecurity; or feeling afraid can too often stop you from taking action toward a goal; or it could be that a phobia prevents you from living a regular life. It may not be entirely obvious to you that fear is the problem because it's your "normal." You may not even define the feeling as fear unless you get really stressed and the emotion can't be ignored, or someone points it out to you. But observe yourself for the next several days and notice how often you feel afraid, insecure, or cautious, even in minor circumstances. For example, my client Shasta would get frightened about her girlfriend's safety if she was late getting home, imagining something terrible had happened to her instead of first thinking of some more realistic reasons for the delay.

2. Lack of Trust

Trust issues are another common sign of disharmony in this Element, and they can show up in various ways. You may find it hard to trust people you're in relationship with, personally or professionally. You may not trust your intuition and so miss out on important guidance from that source of inner knowing. An issue with trust can even equate to lacking a sense of faith in Life overall, unable to believe you'll be supported in finding success. If we can't access feelings of trust, we don't feel safe, and we can view life as full of difficulties we're not sure we'll be able to overcome, rather than believing the universe is a friendly place.

If Water Is Not Your Strongest Element

Even if you don't feel like a very Watery person, there can still be phases in life where you experience a loss of your ability to trust. Elena went through a tumultuous relationship and painful breakup with her fiancé, only to end up feeling she could no longer trust her instincts because she'd made such a terrible choice in the man she'd committed to, as well as how she handled things during their relationship. Another case shows us how this issue can be experienced as a lack of faith after a period of suffering: Channing had been coping with lower back pain for two years, and one day his acupuncturist exclaimed, "You don't have any faith you can heal!" It was a big "Aha!" moment for him as he realized she was right; he had lost trust that his situation could resolve.

If You Are a Water Element Type

If you relate strongly to the Water personality, it could be that you don't fully trust that the person you're in relationship with won't leave you. Abandonment issues are common problems for this Element. For instance, Makayla's husband frequently traveled out of town for work, and while he was away, she insisted he contact her every few hours, or she'd begin to have terrible fantasies that he was never coming back. But issues with trust can be present in more minor ways too. If you notice you're frequently suspicious of other people's motives or wonder if there are things they're not telling you, this can fall into the category of trust issues. You can even be missing a sense of trust in Life itself, as if you don't have faith that, as my beloved friend and founder of Hay House, Louise Hay, would always say, "Life loves you."

3. Loneliness

We can all feel lonely at certain points in time; however, that doesn't necessarily indicate a problem with our Water, because each

Element can feel lonely for different reasons. But only with Water can loneliness be a constant background influence that permeates all your thoughts, emotions, and experiences. It's a very specific type of feeling—a pervasive belief that you're all alone in life, or that no one will ever really know you. This kind of loneliness lives deep in the core of your being, a sense that you are isolated and cut off from the rest of the world, and always will be, and it can subtly affect your daily choices in negative ways, as well as major life decisions.

If Water Is Not Your Strongest Element

If your main personality pattern is not Water, you can of course still feel loneliness in certain circumstances in life. For example, moving to a new city or starting a job where you don't know anyone can cause you to feel lonely and like an outsider; it's a natural reaction. Estele got a fantastic new job in Vienna, but once she arrived, she was overwhelmed by culture shock and language difficulties. She was often misunderstood as she tried to communicate, and some minor social blunders made her start to withdraw. She kept to herself more and more and began to feel like she'd never be able to fit in and be accepted, rather than reminding herself it would be normal to need some time and effort before she gained a sense of belonging in this totally new lifestyle.

If You Are a Water Element Type

If you're a Water person, there's greater potential for you to feel all alone in the world, like "a stranger in a strange land" and very different from other people; or you might have the experience of feeling left out or misunderstood. Lee noticed his colleagues in the office gathering in the conference room for a staff meeting, but he'd not been informed about it. He sat at his desk feeling desolate, certain that they'd purposely left him out. What had actually happened was that an email had gone astray and he never got the notification. But even after he was told about the mistake, he still suspected that was just an excuse to cover up the fact that they'd deliberately ostracized him. And one Water client of mine often complained of being "all alone and lonely" despite the fact that her social calendar was bursting at the seams!

HEALTH ISSUES COMMONLY ASSOCIATED WITH A WATER DISHARMONY

Each of the Five Elements relates to certain organs and functions of the physical system. If there is a health issue associated with something in the list below, this *might* indicate an imbalance with Water Element. You should always consult your medical practitioner about physical health concerns, and you could easily integrate some of the suggestions in this book as part of your treatment plan.

- Kidneys
- Bladder and urinary tract
- Reproductive organs
- Hormones
- Bones and joints (e.g., arthritis, dental problems)
- Lower back pain
- Adrenal glands (e.g., adrenal exhaustion)
- Ears and hearing
- Loss of hair on the head
- Abnormal blood pressure
- Circulation
- Issues with the physical matter of the brain (e.g., brain tumor)

I often observe these health problems in people who have a lot of this Element in their personality patterns, but I also see them in those at the other extreme—people who have very little of it. This is because they can easily forget to take good care of their Water, so it becomes imbalanced. However, it's also true that *anyone* can develop these kinds of health issues, no matter what their Elemental nature. We all have some of this energy in our makeup and therefore need to keep it in the right balance for us. Problems with this Element are telling us it needs some loving attention.

OTHER POSSIBLE SYMPTOMS OF WATER DISHARMONY

The examples described above are ones I frequently see associated with Water Element, but there are many kinds of issues that can reveal a problem with this energy. Some examples of others are:

- Difficulty discerning fact from fantasy
- Melancholy or dark moods
- Extreme obstinacy
- Secretiveness
- Intolerance
- Paranoia or belief in conspiracy theories
- Stalking
- Vindictiveness
- Fear of persecution
- Antisocial behavior
- Controlling; "God complex"
- Sexual obsessions
- Fanaticism
- Feeling impotent
- Loss of will to live
- Con artist; impostor
- Extreme risk-taking

Chapter 6

SIMPLE REMEDIES AND FULL PRESCRIPTION FOR WATER ELEMENT

In some cases, you can easily tell that Water Element is causing a problem with just one current issue in your life and isn't a deeply rooted or long-term imbalance. For that kind of situation, you could try a Simple Remedy approach. If, however, the problem you're dealing with has been an ongoing or more pervasive one, then you should consult the Full Prescription section that follows next.

Before we begin, I'd like to acknowledge that it can feel odd to do these subtle assignments that don't seem to directly address your situation (even though in fact, they do). Unfortunately, our culture has conditioned us to believe that life works in a linear fashion. In other words, if we have a problem, we're taught to target it directly, to figure out how to "fix" it. Or if we have a goal, we should analyze how to get from point A to point B in a direct route, and control the process all along the way. But that's actually not how anything in life works at all. In fact, if you look back in your own experience, how often did you decide on a goal and then directly achieve it in the way you planned?

More often, what actually happens is that something comes out of left field to change things. You attend a workshop, chat with the person sitting next to you, and as a result of that conversation, your life ends up going in an entirely different direction. In other words, life works in curves, not straight lines, and if you try to take a straight-line approach to solve a problem, at best the result will be only a temporary, superficial change. Additionally, your solution often has "side effects" that create new difficulties. And usually, the problem keeps reappearing in new forms, because it wasn't really solved in the first place.

As you work with the following recommendations, you may have to remind yourself that this is based on a science! Even though these may seem like small actions, remember, what you're doing here is applying the equivalent of acupuncture needles, on a whole-life scale. These are purposely designed to be tiny changes, but don't underestimate them—they can activate powerful transformations.

SIMPLE REMEDIES

For any problem, there are always five choices for how to bring balance back. Each of the Elements offers a possible approach for healing, because each has a special relationship to the others. In other words, for every Element, there is one that can nourish it if it's weak, drain it if it's in excess, control it if it's overpowering, or remind it of what *it's* meant to control. And lastly, there is always the option to enhance the Element itself as a remedy.

Interestingly, in Chinese medicine, excess or deficiency in the Elements can look the same. They may exhibit the same kinds of symptoms, cause the same kinds of problems, and even receive similar types of treatment. This means your approach here shouldn't be about figuring out if you have too much Water or too little in the situation you're facing. You can use these remedies for any problem that relates to it. Also, any healthy attention will only help to keep an Element in balance, so you can't go wrong here.

You can select any of the Simple Remedy choices below, or even try all of them if you're not sure which to choose, but I suggest selecting one at first and sticking with it for a while so it has time to take effect.

1. Enhance Water:
Downtime—"Be" and Not "Do"

Whether you're struggling with fear, trust issues, loneliness, or another problem you suspect has to do with Water Element, one approach would be to guide your Water back to health by making "downtime" a priority. But let's define what "downtime" means. It is *not* mindlessly surfing the internet, playing Solitaire on the computer, or spacing out with television!

Downtime is what makes every cell in your body relax and say, "Ahhh." It's the kind of feeling that you get when you have a long soak in the tub, take a nap, get a massage, or meditate, for instance. My client Julia had been feeling blocked by fear and chose the downtime option. She said, "I let myself take a *realllly* long luxurious bath every night this week and I'm astonished that I'm not only refreshed but I feel like I'm getting my mojo back."

For a minimum of five days, every day, take one hour of downtime—more if you can manage it. Don't skip a day and don't take less than one hour! You wouldn't skip a dose of an important medication or take less than prescribed; this should be looked at in the same kind of way.

2. Drain Water with Wood:
Just Do It—Do Something, Anything!

When Water gets out of balance, it can stop flowing and become stagnant. Then it's like you're treading water in life and not going anywhere. Kim had been trying to launch her business for weeks, but she kept stalling and overanalyzing. Eventually, she was so overwhelmed with fear of failure, her mind froze, unable to make decisions. She finally got so angry with herself that she was able to use this remedy. "I took action on one small task each day for a week. And suddenly I was able to make my website live after all this time dragging my feet!"

So, "just do something—anything" means to take some tiny steps toward your goal, even if you don't know whether they're the right ones or if they'll have any effect. The "cure" here is to remind Water Element that its job is to move toward Wood Element. The energy of Wood is about taking action, moving forward, *doing* something, and that can break you right out of your Water stillness in a healthy way. It's not about *what* you do. The fact that you just *do* something gets Water flowing again.

3. Evaporate Water with Fire:
Do Something Crazy—Just Go Have Fun!

An imbalance in Water can make you sink deeper and deeper into your feelings until you just can't find your way out. Then your energy slows down as you get lost stewing in your emotional juices. To counteract this effect, you can bring in the frequency of Fire Element, which Water controls, because it will motivate Water to get moving, and thus get you out of the swamp! Fire excites and stimulates your system, and even a short blast of Fire can be medicine for you.

So get out of the house and do something fun! What crazy, thrilling, or carefree activity lights you up or makes you laugh your head off? For some people, that might be going dancing with friends, or to the latest funny movie. For others, it's a weekend trip out of town, or rolling around on the floor, playing with giggling children. Anything with this kind of energy will break the Watery spell. Chris was feeling down in the dumps and said no to invitations from friends because she knew she'd be "lousy company." She realized her medicine would be to take a day off to do something she loved—going on all the rides at the amusement park!

4. Control Water with Earth:
Reassurance—What Are the Actual Facts Here?

Water gives you imagination, which is a wonderful thing. But at times your imagination may run away with you to create a story in your mind that has little to no basis in reality. Leila's boyfriend didn't return her call, and she started to think he was deliberately ignoring her. And then the story built from there. *He no longer wants to be with me. He's seeing other people and isn't telling me about it. He just doesn't get me and never has. I should never have trusted him, and I'll never trust him again.*

So if you ever suspect you've got a negative fantasy going, one way to break out of it is to give yourself a reality check. In this situation, Leila should ask herself, *What are the actual facts here? He didn't return my call yet. What other facts do I know? He's super busy this week and possibly hasn't had a chance to call. He often forgets to check his voicemail; maybe he hasn't even heard my message yet. This isn't the first time he's taken a few hours to get back to me.* Adding Earth reassurance grounds you back in reality to calm any Watery reaction.

5. Nourish Water with Metal:
Get Inspired—Lift Your Gaze to Look to the Future

Metal can come to the rescue here, to bring the far view, a sense of the big picture, like looking from high above, where our current difficulties shrink to tiny shapes and don't seem so serious. And Metal looks into the future, when our present-day problems will have faded into distant memories. It brings what's most important into focus.

To do this remedy, go somewhere that has a far view. It may be on a hillside where you can gaze miles into the distance, or out a window up high where you can see far, or if nothing else, just look at a picture of a spacious view of the sky and clouds. As you do, imagine what your most ideal future life would be, and how it would feel to actually be living that way. What do you look like in that perfect future? What are you wearing? Where are you standing? Who's there with you? What are you about to go do? Mark did this exercise and said, "First, it felt like I could take a deep breath for the first time in days, and afterward, I realized the right thing to do about my problem, which had been evading me for weeks."

FULL FIVE-ELEMENT PRESCRIPTION TO REMEDY LONG-STANDING WATER ELEMENT ISSUES

If you believe that your Water Element is not just temporarily in need of help, but has been causing problems in your life over a long period of time, then instead of a Simple Remedy approach, you should aim for a Full Prescription that you carry out every day for one month. For example, if you recognize that trust issues have been a pattern in all your relationships, or you are well acquainted with fear as a frequent visitor in your life, then you'd choose this plan to bring your Water back to health.

Here, rather than choosing one of the other four Elements, we focus on enhancing your Water, to lavish it with love and attention, so it grows healthier as a result. Below is a list of recommendations, all of which will act like acupuncture needles to bring healing to your Water, whether it's too active or not active enough.

This is not a lifelong prescription; instead, apply it every day for one month and then see how you feel. Think of this like medicine you'd take to help an illness resolve. You don't need to do everything on this list! I suggest starting off with three or four that appeal to you, and then if you want to, you can add in more or change to different ones as you like. If any these ideas go against your tastes and preferences, or are things your doctor said not to do, then of course don't do them.

Add Water to Your Wardrobe

Each Element has a certain energetic frequency that resonates with a specific color, and for Water, the color is black. So one choice to boost Water in your life is to wear more black, if you like how you look in black. You don't have to dress like an undertaker! Even wearing little touches of black will have an effect.

Or you could dress in a more Watery way with flowing, unstructured clothes, long skirts or loose pants, sensual fabrics like velvet, or dramatic styles with unusual designs. Water-type shoes are flat and can be easily kicked off so your feet feel free!

Create a Watery Environment

The color black can be used in the décor of your home and office as well. Add some black in each room of the house in little ways, such as placing a black pillow on the couch or hanging a black towel in the bathroom.

You might add artwork to your space that has black in it, or that shows scenes of water like a lake, river, or the ocean, or that has fluid, wavy lines. Or place some actual water there, such as a fountain, aquarium, or a bowl of water with decorative rocks, or a flower floating in it.

Water Element has to do with darkness, so you could install dimmer switches on the lights to create more mood lighting, or turn on a table lamp rather than the overhead lights. For a really Watery touch, turn off all the lights and just use candlelight!

Do Watery Activities

Seek Water

Literally spending more time in or near water is a remedy! Soak in the tub, go swimming, walk along the shore, go to the beach, have a session in a float tank; anything to do with water will be good for you here.

Practice Nonlinear Living

Water is about ease and flow; in nature, water moves in curves, not straight lines. For you, that means freeing yourself from a linear, structured lifestyle as much as possible over the next month. For example, when you go grocery shopping, don't take a list. Or if that's too extreme, take your list, but once you've gotten everything on it, don't leave the store. Instead, linger and explore. Make it an adventure; find some exotic new ingredient you've never used before, or wander the aisles to discover foods you hadn't thought of trying. You don't necessarily have to buy them! The point of this activity is about free flow.

If you go for a walk, don't have any particular destination in mind. You might explore a new neighborhood or wander through a local park. And look for opportunities to escape from a strict, regimented schedule in your daily life. Over the next month, as much as you can, give yourself more freedom, rather than adhering to a rigid daily calendar.

Exercise

Any workout that includes slow, fluid movement will be a match here. Examples are yoga, tai chi, qi gong, ice skating, roller skating, skiing, or slow dancing.

Get Horizontal

You can position yourself in a Watery way by being horizontal. That could mean working while you're stretched out in bed, or lying down on the couch to read or watch a movie. And of course, sinking into the bathtub for a long soak would be the most Watery way to get horizontal!

Listen to Silence or Music

Silence is associated with Water, but so is music because Water Element relates to the ears and hearing. So if you feel the noise around you at home or work is stressing your system, you might give yourself a break and go somewhere quiet. Or you might put on your headphones and lose yourself in the world of your favorite music. However, Water types of music are more slow and relaxing than peppy and stimulating, so make sure you choose something that has the right vibration. Listening to a guided meditation or the sounds of water (e.g., recordings of ocean waves or a rushing river) would be another option here as well.

Choose Downtime

Probably the single most important thing you could do to boost your Water Element is daily downtime. In our culture, hardly anyone takes true downtime. It's not hanging out on social media or playing computer games or zoning out watching videos. You may think these are helping you relax but they're not actually replenishing your energy. Downtime is when every cell in your body relaxes with a deep, grateful sigh! It's a long soak in the tub, a nap, a massage, meditation, or just gazing out the window and daydreaming. (By the way, worrying, analyzing, and ruminating do not equal daydreaming!)

Incorporate 30 to 60 minutes of real downtime into your daily life for the next month without fail, and more if you can manage to.

Cultivate Dreamtime

Dreamtime can be when you let your creative juices flow to paint, write, sketch, play an instrument, create crafts, or whatever you enjoy doing that's creative. But you also move into a state of dreamtime when you allow yourself to daydream, fantasize, let your imagination run free. For example, where in the world would you love to visit? Research or imagine the entire trip and let your fantasies have no limits, because this isn't about making decisions or planning an actual trip but simply being in a state of daydreaming.

Dreamtime could also include keeping a dream journal. If you don't usually remember your dreams, start a practice of scribbling any little shred of a memory of a dream, or recording on your phone, even if you can barely remember anything. Your system will soon get trained to remember more and more and soon you'll be downloading entire dreams each morning that could have important intuitive messages for you.

Practice Reality-Free Living

Water Element relates to nighttime, when we're asleep, awash in our dreams and not in touch with the real world. So another way to boost Water in your life is to read fiction, not nonfiction books (except for this one—grin!). Watch more movies, and fewer documentaries, news channels, or reality shows. Listen to music, not podcasts, unless they're ones that tell fictional stories.

Find Solitude

Water is the time before birth and after death, when we're not connected to other human beings. So another way to immerse yourself in Water is to get more time alone. Find space each day for the next month for quiet solitude, where you're all alone. You get extra points for doing something Watery during that time, such as meditating, listening to music, bathing, etc.!

Engage Your Intuition

Water is what puts you in touch with that wise inner voice that guides you in ways that are beyond logic and left-brained analysis. When your Water is out of balance, you may not be listening to those important messages from deep inside your soul. Or you may not be able to discern what's a true intuitive hit from what's just your imagination.

One practice would be to trust your intuition more for the next month, but to do it in little ways, and about things that won't matter if you're wrong. In other words, don't buy a car just based on a feeling! For example, if you visit a news website every day, before you log on, tune in and see if you can get any sense of what the headline will be about, or what colors or images might be in today's photo. Then log on and check if your impressions bear any relation at all to what's actually on your screen. Even the vaguest similarity can be a hit. If you thought of what seemed to be a bald-headed man, but the actual photo is of a sports dome, well, that rounded surface of the dome matches your impression!

You might also read books or take courses about intuition, or get a reading from an intuitive advisor. Anything that gives you more access to this valuable source of information and guidance will be good for your Water.

Align with the Magic Hours for Water

Through thousands of years of research, Chinese medicine discovered cyclic biorhythms that our bodies move through in each 24-hour period. Every few hours, we enter a different phase related to one of the Elements. The powerful phase for Water begins at 3 P.M. and lasts till 7 P.M. each day. Considering that Water has to do with rest and replenishment, is it a surprise that midafternoon is often when we hit the wall and experience a noticeable dip in energy? Around 3:00 or soon after, people reach for coffee, chocolate, or some other stimulant to keep going, or they slow way down and start watching the clock for the time they can leave work and go home.

To align with this natural schedule, make time for even a brief rest between the hours of 3 and 7 P.M. It could even be as short as a 20-minute power nap or meditation, or just gazing out the window and letting your mind wander without feeling guilty.

Increase Water Element Foods in Your Diet

Staying well hydrated by drinking plenty of water is a given for this treatment, of course, but aside from that, the absolute best change you could make to your diet if you want to boost the energy of Water in your life is to have more soup. It's chock-full of natural salts and minerals that vibrate at the Water frequency. Any kind of soup is fine, but bone broth gets extra points because Water Element relates to the bones. Eating more fish, seafood, and kelp helps as well because they literally come from the water.

Water Practice: Ancestors' Blessings

Chinese culture brings us some important wisdom here in the concept of "ancestors." You may have heard that in China, they "honor the ancestors," or you may have seen an altar in a Chinese business or home with incense or offerings to the ancestors. But this is a much richer and deeper concept than most Westerners realize.

The Chinese believe that when a family member dies and passes over, they lose their sometimes troublesome earthly personality and become a beneficent Ancestor, who beams blessings to the family from the other side. These blessings consist of all the wisdom and power that they gained through their lives, which now become a loving transmission to the remaining family members, to support them in their journey.

However, in the West, we don't have this conviction. We believe we're all on our own and it's up to us to forge our ways in life, purely on our own willpower. But this very belief is a major contributing factor in the plague of exhaustion these days, everyone draining their own inner strength just to make it through. If only we were open to receiving those ancestral blessings, we could ride a powerful tide of support and move forward with so much less effort on our part!

This Water Element practice helps us do that. Anything you do to turn your attention to your ancestry can be healing now. For instance, Water has to do with traits and tendencies inherited from your forebears, and we know it's not unusual for things to run in families, such as a natural artistic talent or an interest in a particular hobby or profession. So if you can identify any interests or talents that you share with any of your ancestors, make time for it this month, no matter what it is, even if previously you thought it was a waste of time. Not only will it stimulate and enhance your Water power here, it may surprise you by becoming a more significant part of your life than you first expected!

Overall, pay more attention to things that have to do with your lineage. For instance, you could go through old photo albums, cook traditional family recipes, research your genealogy, visit older relatives to hear their stories, or take flowers to the cemetery where family members are buried. You might research or travel to the country or countries of your heritage.

Some people who came from a very dysfunctional family may feel an aversion to turning their attention to anything to do with their ancestors because it can trigger a flood of painful memories. If this is your situation, it can help to remind yourself that as each family member passed to the other side, they were cleansed of their toxic personalities; their only influence now is one of love and support. However, if this is still too difficult for you to accept right now, you may want to choose to do things that are more about your heritage and less directly connected to those relatives. So instead of talking about old family stories, you might choose to cook recipes from your culture or research the locations from which your forebears emigrated.

Connecting more with the energy of ancestors can start a flood of blessings appearing in your life in mysterious ways. You may begin to feel like you're being carried on the current rather than fighting to swim upstream!

But everything has two sides, and when it comes to ancestors, there is also the possibility of detrimental influences. For example, if someone in your family line experienced a trauma that they weren't able to recover from, it could become an inherited issue. This means that trauma can be passed down through the DNA of subsequent generations, causing a problem in each of their lives. The issue may look like that descendant's personal problem, but no matter how they try to solve it, nothing works—because the problem didn't originate with them. Even Western science is now studying this issue through the developing field of epigenetics, where it's been proven that emotional trauma can be passed down to affect descendants. For example, people whose ancestors lived through the Holocaust in World War II are far more likely to have PTSD (post-traumatic stress disorder) even if they never personally experienced trauma in their own lives.

If you feel an inherited issue is involved with a problem you have, any of the recommendations in the Prescription in this chapter can be healing. They will open your system to the positive blessings beaming from those in your entire lineage and thus cleanse inherited imbalances. You might also try a session with a reputable psychic medium to see if you could communicate with any relatives who have passed; sometimes healing can be done on the other side through that process. Or you might keep a record of your dreams in case there are helpful interactions or messages available there. Also consider having a Family Constellations session with a practitioner you trust. (This form of energy work specifically addresses disharmonies passed down through the family field.) You might look into "ancestral clearing," which is a method I teach that clears and balances the energy back through the generations on both sides of your family. (See the Recommended Resources section.)

As your Water Element heals, you regain power, not only in terms of vitality, but also in increased trust—in yourself, in others, and in Life. With greater access to your intuitive wisdom, you're less and less blocked by fear and insecurity. You can summon the courage to face the unknown with a limitless supply of strength and willpower. And you feel yourself moving forward almost like a leaf floating on the stream, being carried on the current with no effort on your part.

Important note: After using any of the treatments listed in the Simple Remedies or the Full Prescription, don't cling tightly to what you *think* the results should be. When you're back in alignment with the natural flow, your life will rearrange itself in ways that may surprise you! But if you're focused on what you think *should* happen, you may not notice the doors that are opening to you. Trust the process and welcome what comes.

Chapter 7

WOOD ELEMENT AND SYMPTOMS OF WOOD IMBALANCES— ANGER, DEPRESSION, LACK OF FORGIVENESS, AND HEALTH ISSUES

Let's review what we know about Wood Element: it's the phase in the cycle when the life force actually enters the world—the baby is born, sprouts break through the soil in the spring, and we come to waking consciousness in the morning, after a deep sleep.

We can understand Wood energy by thinking of the little child, with their go-go-go attitude throughout the day, running and shouting. All the adults say, "I wish I had their energy!" Small children embody Wood's natural enthusiasm, throwing themselves into everything, sometimes impulsively so.

We can recognize it in the essence of spring, when life bursts forth with a powerful vitality, a drive to grow and grow. In the spring, we regain a more optimistic outlook, and feel stirred to grow in our lives in some way too, such as taking a class or deciding on a change we want to make.

And Wood can be seen in how we are in the morning, diving in to get some work done. At this time of day, we're planning our to-do list and getting ourselves organized. We don't dillydally; we get down to business!

We can get a good sense of Wood's characteristics by observing it in nature too. There is a well-organized plan imprinted in a tree that directs its growth; a distinct vision for where it's headed: up and up.

Chinese medicine teaches that Wood Element empowers us to define who we are, and what we stand for. It helps us create a vision for the direction we want to go in life and gives us the drive to achieve it. It allows us the clarity of mind to think logically and create a good plan, and then to take decisive action based on that plan. Wood energy acts like a booster rocket to give us liftoff and the confidence to keep going till we reach our goal. And most of all, it imbues us with a deep desire to work hard to make the world a better place.

Even if you didn't recognize much Wood in your nature when you took the survey, you still do have some of this Element, of course. It's likely you'll disregard it, however, in favor of the other energies that you relate to more, which can cause Wood to fall out of balance and create problems in your life. For example, Fatima had a lot of Water in her nature but very little Wood Element. She had dreams of working in computer animation, but she couldn't find any jobs in that field. She said, "It's as if I could see where I wanted to go, and I started in that direction, but then things just stalled." Without healthy Wood energy, you'll lack the ability to figure out all the steps to get from here to there.

If, however, your personality is Wood energy, it may at times have too much influence on you, and cause as many problems as when it's not so active. Stephen felt so driven to prove himself to the world that he focused intensely on earning as much money as possible in his new business. There's nothing wrong with being financially successful! But in his zeal, he pushed his employees far too hard, and refused requests to discuss office problems because it was a waste of his time "to have to sit and listen to them whine." But because those issues didn't get addressed, turnover in the office skyrocketed as the staff got frustrated, and then more things went wrong as so many new employees made mistakes. This made customers unhappy, of course, and his profits plummeted—the exact opposite of what he was trying to achieve.

So no matter how much Wood is a part of your personal design, if this Element goes out of balance in your life, there will be problems! Let's move on to look at three common issues that disharmonies in Wood create, and then discover ways to solve these difficulties by bringing balance back to the whole.

THREE COMMON SYMPTOMS OF WOOD IMBALANCE

1. Anger

The emotion that relates to Wood Element is anger, a feeling we usually only think of in negative terms. But Chinese medicine teaches that every emotion has two sides: one that is detrimental and one that is beneficial. We usually see anger expressed in destructive ways, like when someone shouts in rage and hurts another's feelings, or furiously strikes out and causes damage. But anger can be used in positive ways too. This feeling is actually just a reaction to a situation we think is wrong and should be changed. It activates our energy to speak up, to take action, to create a breakthrough. Anger can actually be a positive drive to help us change.

If your anger is expressed in unhealthy ways, it's destructive, of course. But a less obvious way anger can cause problems is in too *much* drive—for example, being a workaholic or compulsive exerciser. And at the other end of the range, if you judge your anger as wrong and try to suppress it, this will cut you off from your positive Wood energy. Results can be a loss of confidence, feeling stuck in life, or a lack of assertiveness, which leads to weak boundaries and letting people take advantage of you. When you bring this energy into balance, you're able to manage your anger appropriately so you can initiate effective change whenever necessary.

If Wood Is Not Your Strongest Element

Anyone can struggle with anger at times, whether or not Wood is a major pattern in their personality. We all go through phases when we're dealing with some degree of frustration—if not full-on anger—due to a difficult situation, and it can so easily knock our energy out of balance if we don't find a healthy outlet for that feeling. There can also be times when we have problems accessing our positive anger when we need to. Kathy had an Earth personality, which made her too concerned about upsetting anyone. This prevented her from speaking up about a problem with her team at work, and as a result, what could have been easily corrected developed over time into a major backlog. We need to be able to call up our Wood anger so we can change what's wrong!

If You Are a Wood Element Type

There's always a spectrum for every emotion, and for anger, at one end of the range is mild impatience, then growing to irritation, then frustration, then eventually anger, and at the far end of the spectrum will be pure rage. Most Wood people will only experience the milder versions of anger on a regular basis. But if you find you're too easily frustrated, or if you get outright angry in situations that don't call for it, this Element is probably out of balance. However, in some cases, it's the *lack* of anger that's the problem for Wood people. Hanna was a Wood woman but raised by a rageful father, and as a result, did everything to avoid ever experiencing that emotion again, even inside of herself. But this stifled her drive in life and was the reason she was stuck in a job that was "safe" but that she hated.

2. Depression

Healthy Wood energy is outward-moving but if it becomes unhealthy, it may turn to move in the opposite direction: inward. Even Western psychology has defined depression as "anger turned inward," and Chinese medicine shows us how this can happen. Healthy Wood energy gives us a "can do" attitude, an optimism born of a natural sense that we're able to achieve our goals. But if we aim for something and fail, it can put a dent in that confidence. If a lot of little failures accumulate, or even if there's one major defeat, we can blame ourselves; in other words, our Wood anger is directed inward to form depression and, eventually, hopelessness and apathy.

If Wood Is Not Your Strongest Element

Even if you don't feel Wood energy is a big part of who you are, it's inevitable that in life, things don't always turn out as you hoped. The promotion you wanted goes to someone else, or every publisher turns down the manuscript you worked so hard on, and you may begin to find your spirits dropping. Jessica had big plans for earning her master's degree at a prestigious university abroad but didn't get accepted. She said she'd had such high hopes for this feather in her cap to impress future employers that when she got the news, her whole world just came crashing down. She felt totally discouraged and dragged around for months afterward, unable to think of what else she might do at this point in her life.

If You Are a Wood Element Type

If you're a Wood person, it may not be that you ever encounter a time of depression in your life. But if you do, it can be far more difficult than for other types because that desire to succeed, to not be a "loser," is such a strong influence that even a little defeat can balloon into a huge issue, causing you to lose hope, which diminishes your natural drive. Many Wood people get depressed after feeling "blocked" by someone, as if that person were deliberately preventing their progress. Sophia's boss refused to assign her a project she requested, and she felt he was purposely keeping her from rising through the ranks at work. Her first reaction was to get angry and argue, but that just made him hold a grudge and turn down her other proposals, and she eventually gave up and fell into depression.

3. Lack of Forgiveness

When I do readings for people, I often feel like I'm translating for them what another person meant that my client had been misjudging. We all tend to assume others think the same way we do, but that couldn't be further from the truth, and this guarantees misunderstandings. And sometimes these result in hurt and anger that, if not resolved, can cause us to blame the other person without trying to understand why this happened, and so prevents us from reaching a place where we can forgive. There's usually an aspect of self-blame in these circumstances too, which is another form of lack of forgiveness—of self. Each time forgiveness is an issue, our Wood energy is encumbered and not able to maintain a healthy flow.

If Wood Is Not Your Strongest Element

You don't have to be a Wood person to have ever felt mistreated or misjudged, and sometimes this can be hard to get over. When anger can't find a way to transform into forgiveness, those feelings will start to adversely affect us, first on the level of the spirit, then emotionally, and eventually physically. Maggie was in a terribly dysfunctional marriage and her divorce was torture because her husband tried everything he could to punish her. She carried her outrage for years, unable to let it go, until finally her lack of forgiveness manifested physically with a gallbladder attack. In Chinese medicine, the gallbladder is a Wood Element organ, so we can understand why this part of her body was affected, not only by her inability to forgive her ex-husband, but also herself. We are often unaware of how much we also blame ourselves for letting others hurt us.

If You Are a Wood Element Type

In some cases, a Wood person's natural confidence and desire to grow gets thwarted by mistreatment from someone who has power over them in life. Richard was a Wood type whose father was angry and controlling, and was hard on his son, believing he should toughen him up and "make a man out of him." He purposely belittled the boy and looked for every opportunity to shame him and cut him down. As an adult, Richard was the opposite of what we'd expect a Wood person to be like. He was timid and hesitant, cut off from the healthy assertiveness this Element was meant to provide him; his Wood power had been severely injured due to his father's abuse. He carried deep anger toward his father, but hadn't recognized the need to understand how terribly damaged emotionally the man was, which could then lead him to find forgiveness and thus regain his power.

HEALTH ISSUES COMMONLY ASSOCIATED WITH A WOOD DISHARMONY

Each of the Five Elements relates to certain organs and functions of the physical system. If there is a health issue with any in the following list, this *might* indicate an imbalance with Wood Element. You should always consult your medical practitioner about physical health concerns, and you could easily integrate some of the suggestions in this book as part of your treatment plan.

- Liver
- Gallbladder
- Headaches and migraines
- Neck and shoulders (e.g., tension, injury)
- Tendons and ligaments
- Jaw (e.g., jaw injury, TMJ, grinding teeth)
- Vision and eye function
- Addictive tendencies
- Acid reflux and gastroesophageal reflux disease (GERD)
- Distractibility (e.g., attention deficit disorder)
- Bulimia
- Cramps, twitches, Tourette syndrome

In my experience, people with a Wood personality tend to have these kinds of health issues, but it's possible to find them in other types who have imbalances in this Element too. No matter what your particular combination of Elements, you could develop issues with this energy because everyone has some of it in their design. Wood Element problems are telling us it needs healing.

OTHER POSSIBLE SYMPTOMS OF WOOD DISHARMONY

The problems described above are the ones I most frequently see associated with a Wood Element imbalance, but there are many others that can reveal an issue with this energy. Some others are:

- Competitive
- Defensive (e.g., difficulty admitting fault, or blaming others)
- Aggressive, hostile, confrontational
- Compulsive behavior
- Overly regimented
- Indecisive
- Procrastination
- Self-harming tendencies
- Impulse-control problems
- Issues with authority
- Passivity or lack of confidence
- Feelings of shame
- Feeling under attack or caught in a trap
- Hyperfocused
- Argumentative or sarcastic
- Feeling ungrounded
- Lack of discipline

Chapter 8

SIMPLE REMEDIES AND FULL PRESCRIPTION FOR WOOD ELEMENT

If you see you're currently dealing with a Wood Element problem but it isn't one that has kept recurring in your life, it's probably just a temporary imbalance and can be addressed with a Simple Remedy approach in the section below. If, however, you recognize what you're dealing with is just version 7.0 of a long-time problem, you'll want to use the steps in the section after this, the Full Prescription.

SIMPLE REMEDIES

You always have five choices for bringing an Element back into balance because each of these energies has a certain healing influence. We can find four remedies by using the Nourishing and Control Cycles, and a choice for the fifth is enhancing the Element itself.

You can try any or all of the recommendations below, but not at the same time. Begin with one and give it a chance to process for several days. Remember these small steps are the equivalent of acupuncture needles activating a certain kind of energy in your life that is needed to transform your situation, so don't underestimate their power to create change for you.

1. Enhance Wood:
Get Moving—Exercise Out in Nature

Wood not only needs an outlet for all its drive, it also must keep that vitality activated, and one of the best treatments for supporting healthy drive is to exercise. Even Western medicine recommends exercise as a treatment for depression, and in many cases, it's been found to be as effective as medication. However, this remedy is not only for depression—it's a fit for any kind of Wood problem. I advise that you do any exercise outdoors, as nature is especially healing for Wood, because that's where the green growing things are—all Wood energy!

Nick was dealing with a situation at work that just made his blood boil. His new supervisor seemed intent on making his life hell. She openly criticized Nick in front of his colleagues, and when he tried to impress her with an idea for getting new clients, the supervisor presented it to her boss and took credit for it! Nick recognized how toxic his anger was to his system and decided to use this "cure" of exercise. For 10 days, he went for a run before and after work and was amazed to discover his supervisor backing off and not targeting him anymore. With his Wood energy back in balance, she sensed she could no longer pick on him.

2. Move Wood toward Fire:
Encourage—Be a Cheerleader for a Friend

One way to return Wood to health is to get it moving in the right direction—toward Fire. That Element is bright and positive, which may not be how you're feeling right now. But you *can* access it if it's to help another person. In other words, you probably know someone who could use a little encouragement in some way. Act as a cheerleader for them, point out their positive qualities, applaud each minor accomplishment, and boost their confidence each step of the way.

Kris had been depressed for weeks when she made friends with Aiko at an art class. She was amazed at how naturally talented Aiko was, and when she learned she was applying for a grant so she could concentrate on creating an exhibition, she wanted to help. Aiko was daunted by the requirements of the grant application, but Kris kept her optimistic through that process. Once Aiko got the grant, Kris continued to be a cheerleader for her as she created the art, dispelling her self-doubt every step of the way. As Aiko reached her goal, Kris found her depression had dissipated. She'd unknowingly used the power of Fire Element to heal.

3. Focus Wood toward Earth:
Eat—Cook for Friends, or Eat Out Together

Wood controls Earth, so if we stimulate Earth energy, Wood starts to do more of the right thing. Earth Element is about nourishment and digestion, and it's interesting that people who feel depressed often turn to food for comfort. Perhaps on an unconscious level, this is their system trying to rebalance by boosting their Earth. However, just eating doesn't help! There is a more complete cure: Earth has to do with feeding others as well as yourself, and feeling a sense of community when doing so.

So the recommendation here is to invite a friend or friends over for a home-cooked meal, or if you don't like to cook, then go out for some meals with them and enjoy both the food and the company. Gail was job hunting without any luck and she started feeling really discouraged. Too often, she found herself on the couch at night in her sweats, making a meal of chips and dip, feeling too hopeless to make the effort to cook anything. One night she spontaneously accepted a neighbor's invitation to come over for dinner. They had such a nice time cooking together that they began trading off, one night at each apartment, and Gail's mood started to lift. Shortly afterward, she got two job offers!

4. Control Wood with Metal:
Purification—Clean Up Your Diet

In this remedy, we're talking about meals again but in a different way. Metal is about purity, so for the next several days, avoid fast food. Try to eat organically as much as you can, and drink filtered water. But watch out for being too rigid with food. Metal is also about sensual pleasure, so enjoy your meals! Purification can also be translated as beautification, so why not use your best china, arrange your food on the plate in an attractive way, and put flowers on the table?

There's an additional step you can take here too. Wood energy creates tension in the body in certain places, one of them being the jaw. Wood personalities tend to like crunchy foods like celery or chips because they enjoy the feeling of biting down hard. So for this Metal remedy, it's best to avoid foods that make your jaw tense up. Strengthening Metal in this way can break you out of focusing on things that aren't really important and let you see what's truly valuable. Lucas was procrastinating about a decision, and after changing his diet in this way, he sat right down one morning to write a "Pro and Con" list and made his choice.

5. Nourish Wood with Water:
Saturate—Add Images and Sounds of Water

When your Wood Element is in distress, Water can come to the rescue. Surround yourself with things that represent water—for example, artwork with images of water, or recordings of ocean waves or rainstorms, or place a bowl of water with a flower floating in it on the dining room table at dinner. Look online for images of water during breaks from work, or research beach vacations!

Kylie had escaped an abusive marriage and was trying to figure out her next step. But she had been so beaten down by her dominating husband that she felt totally defeated, and unable to summon the mental clarity to figure out how to start her life over. When every day for the past seven years had been a battle to fend off her aggressor, her Wood was exhausted, and so her ability to think and plan, and to have confidence so she could begin anew was seriously depleted. At first it seemed impossible to her that a brief period of flooding her life with Water could have much effect, but she gave it a try and reported that each day brought more of a sense that "Maybe I *can* do this!"

FULL FIVE-ELEMENT PRESCRIPTION TO REMEDY LONG-STANDING WOOD ELEMENT ISSUES

When Wood Element hasn't just been out of balance for the short-term, but you see it's created problems in your life for years or a single difficulty relating to Wood keeps coming back, then you should use a more complete Full Prescription that you carry out for a full month. For example, if you've always struggled with anger, or depression is not new for you, you'd choose this method, just like you'd take a course of medicine to treat a persistent ailment.

Remember that here, instead of using any of the other Elements, a Full Prescription works on enhancing all aspects of your Wood energy to bring it back to a healthy balance again. In most cases, you can use this Full Prescription whether you feel your Wood is in the driver's seat in your life too often or if you believe it's depleted and not functioning powerfully enough. This is not only because excess and deficiency often look the same and are treated in the same manner, but also because any positive attention given to an Element will help it, either way.

This Full Prescription is meant to be applied each day for one full month. Select as many of the following choices as you like, but remember that you don't have to do all of them. Begin with three or four and you can add more or switch to others as you go if you want to. The most important thing is to not choose any that don't fit your own tastes or ones that go against your doctor's advice.

Add Wood to Your Wardrobe

The color associated with Wood is green, so one choice to bring balance to this energy is to wear any shade of green. You can add it in small touches, such as a scarf, and it can range from muted tones like olive all the way to bright green if you like that shade.

You could also dress in way that's more aligned with Wood energy, which is practical clothing that you don't have to fuss with, and that lets you be active. Wood-type shoes are ones you can easily walk or run in, and for women, if you have to wear heels, they'd be chunky low ones with a squared-off toe. Hairstyles would be easy-care kinds that don't require styling. Wash-and-go is Wood!

Create a Wood Environment

Green can be added to the décor of your home and workplace as well. Put a green vase on a table, or use a green coffee cup, for example, and don't forget houseplants (not flowers) as a perfect representation of live Wood energy! You might want to add artwork that has green in it, or images of trees. Look for ways you can add a bit of green to every room.

The shape for Wood is a vertical rectangle, reminiscent of a tree, so adding tall rectangular objects like art in long vertical frames is one option, or candlesticks on a table is another. Wood home décor has the overall feel of a hunting lodge or log cabin. Furniture made of wood is certainly a fit, but no fussy doilies on the tables or tchotchkes on the shelves! A Wood Element environment looks well organized and free of clutter.

Do Wood Activities

Create a Vision Board

Wood has to do with desire, what we want in life, and what direction we plan to go in to get it. When Wood is out of balance, we can struggle with finding clarity on this kind vision. To help with this, create a vision board with pictures that represent something—anything—you desire. Print out images from the internet, clip them from magazines, or create them yourself. The pictures can be of material things you'd love to have, like a car, or they can be images of activities you'd like to do, such as travel, or scenes that represent ways you'd like to feel, like a cozy night at home. The point here is actually not about finding a goal or getting the things in the pictures you choose. And neither is it an exercise in "attraction" or manifesting. (Frankly, what we think we want at any point in life is merely a reflection of our current level of imbalance!) Instead, this practice boosts Wood energy and starts to form a future that is a better fit for you.

Stay Active

Wood is the Element that likes to be active physically, so work out as often as possible and try not to skip more than one day of exercise. The best kinds of exercise for Wood are any that challenge you and require effort, such as strength training, power walking, running, hiking, climbing, Pilates, or competitive sports. If you don't like team sports, you could compete with yourself—for instance, trying to beat your best time. And because nature is specifically healing for Wood energy, try to do these activities outdoors—especially around trees, the physical representation of this Element!

Get Organized

Wood excels at creating efficient and practical systems, so this would be a great time to get things in order. For example, organize your files, arrange your books in alphabetical order or by subject, and clear any clutter. If you're struggling with clutter, this would be a good time to hire a professional organizer to help you with the process. Most have Wood personalities, so they'll bring this energy directly into your home!

Garden and Do Yardwork

Wood "breaks up" Earth Element, so digging in the garden is definitely a Wood activity! Add new plants and clean out garden clutter. If it's not the season when you can do that, organize your gardening tools to prepare for the spring, and research seeds and plants so you can create a new plan for your garden, which will stimulate that good Wood energy of thinking and strategizing.

Fix or Build

This is an excellent time to make little repairs around the house, because Wood is "fixing" energy. They should be short-term projects, however; not some long, drawn-out job. Change a lightbulb, or mend a piece of clothing, for instance. Building something would also fit in this category—for example, putting together an IKEA bookcase or even playing LEGO with your child.

Restructure Your To-Do List

You may already make to-do lists, but there's a special type that is uniquely tailored to this Full Prescription. There are two steps: First, create a brand-new list every day, and even if you didn't get much done on the previous day's list, don't recycle it. For this purpose, you can even include tasks you'd normally do anyhow without needing a reminder, such as eating lunch or taking out the trash. Second, each time you complete something on that list, be sure to take a moment and cross it off, with a victorious feeling of *There—it's done!* These two acts of starting over fresh each day and of acknowledging that a job—no matter how minor—is successfully done is healing for Wood.

Make Noise

This Element relates to making a loud noise in some way so we can use that here to boost its energy. The first choice would be to sound off with your voice; for instance, shouting or singing are options, as is voicing your opinion when you spot a problem instead of not saying anything. You may be surprised at how good it feels. And speak up for yourself too; for example, declare your preference for a restaurant choice at lunch instead of saying, "Whatever you'd like is fine with me!" Look for other opportunities for noisemaking too, especially if it's percussive like drumming or banging tools or pots and pans, or even tapping your fingers as you think because that way of making sound is a match for Wood energy.

Get Linear

Wood energy gifts us with a linear and efficient approach to things, where every action has a beginning, middle, and end. So include as much of that style with your daily activities. For example, if you go for a walk, have a destination in mind and when you reach it, turn around and go straight home; or plan to walk for 20 minutes in one direction and 20 minutes right back again. In other words, don't wander or have an open-ended walk. When you shop for groceries, buy everything on your list but then leave the store.

Don't continue to shop and look for other things to buy. Prepare a schedule for each day, and as much as possible, stick to it. Of course there will be times you have to change your plans and that's no problem; just try to keep most of your day well structured.

Learn Something New

This is the Element that challenges you to grow and develop, so learning something new is another way of reengaging with your Wood energy. Take a course in person or online, or read a how-to book, or teach yourself some new skill by watching videos. It doesn't matter what it is so much as the fact that you're pushing yourself to grow in some way. And once you have that new knowledge, put it to use—do something with it! It's okay if you don't feel confident yet, just test it out, even in a little way, and see what happens.

Get Involved with a Cause

Wood is the energy that empowers us to have firm beliefs and makes us willing to take action, to fight for what we believe in. So to stimulate your Wood energy, choose a cause and get involved. You might volunteer in your community, support a political candidate, raise funds for a charity, or act in some other way to make the world a better place.

Align with the Magic Hours for Wood

Thousands of years before Western medicine developed the concept of the body's biorhythms, Chinese medicine discovered our systems move through daily Elemental patterns, every few hours affected by one of these five energies. The essential phase for Wood begins at 11 P.M. and ends at 3 A.M. each night.

If you're asleep during that time, your unconscious will naturally process problems and decisions, and deliver insights on what to do. You've heard people say "Let me sleep on it" when you're asking them for a decision, or you may have experienced struggling with how to handle an issue and then after a good night's sleep, the next day it occurs to you exactly what to do about it. This is the result of your Wood Element helping you make that decision effortlessly, while you were slumbering during this phase of time.

But if you aren't asleep during those hours, you may not only end up having trouble making decisions or solving problems. You could feel stuck in life, finding it difficult to move forward, mysteriously stymied at reaching a goal, or not even be able to create a vision for what you want next in life. So it's an incredibly important time of night, and the general rule is to be in bed with your eyes closed by 11 P.M. at the latest. If you have to make some minor adjustments in your evening schedule in order to do this, I promise you won't regret it!

(If you have to work a night shift and it's simply not possible to be asleep during those hours, I hope you can rectify that and find work that allows you to have a healthier schedule. But for now, if you simply have to be awake between 11 P.M. and 3 A.M., then use that time to focus on thinking, planning, and making decisions. It won't be as effective but at least you'll be aligning yourself with the energy of this phase!)

Increase Wood Element Foods in Your Diet

This Element benefits the most from a very clean diet, so if you can reduce or eliminate sugar, processed food, alcohol, and other drugs during this time, you'll be giving it good care. Supportive foods are dark green leafy vegetables, celery, asparagus, berries, and liver. Foods that have a sour flavor, such as citrus fruits, fermented vegetables like sauerkraut, or vinegary foods like pickles are also beneficial. Keep to a structured schedule of meals; don't skip any, and no eating in the car or over the sink! Sit down when you eat, and don't be in a rush.

Wood Practice: Individuation

The spiritual principles of Chinese medicine teach that Wood Element has to do with individuation, the process of defining who you are, where you stand, what you believe in, and what path you plan to take in life. It gives you a firm sense of self, based on your own personal truths rather than an acceptance of standards imposed by authority figures. This creates a healthy confidence, and makes you feel firmly rooted, like a tree. But it also gives you the flexibility to change your mind when you learn new information, just like plants are able to adjust the direction they grow in order to get the most sunlight.

Individuation is always an ongoing process, happening in different ways at various stages in life. Babies undergo this experience as they begin to realize they are separate from their mothers, children as they enter school, and adolescents as they pull away from their parents. But it continues throughout our adult lives, in relationships, careers, spiritual paths, and how we journey into aging, always redefining what the plan should be from here, and how to stand firm for who we know ourselves to be.

The following two exercises can help support your personal individuation at this stage in your life. They can give you greater confidence in who you are and why, because of the battles you've fought and the victories you attained, that makes you the strong, competent person you are now.

Exercise 1: Take some time to define yourself by answering the three questions below. You might simply make a long list, or journal about these topics, or create a more official statement of beliefs.

- What are my personal truths; what do I believe in?
- Who do I know myself to be at this point in my life?
- How do I see my mission in life at this stage?

Exercise 2: Create a timeline of your life, spelling out the growth and change that's taken place from the very beginning to the current year. Start out by listing the date and location you were born, and then any significant years things changed, such as when a sibling was born, or you started school, or your family moved to a new house. Write down the points in childhood when you remember certain achievements, such as learning to ride a bike, or making a new friend. Include any specific challenges such as if your parents divorced, because even difficulties eventually help us emerge with a stronger sense of self. Then continue with the timeline into your adult life, listing the years that important changes happened, as well as both your challenges and accomplishments along the way, until you reach the present day.

As your Wood regains power, you'll have more clarity about decisions, and fewer problems with procrastination or self-doubt. You'll feel more confident in your own skin, and not so affected by other people's judgments. A greater flexibility will emerge, allowing you to adapt as you need to, without getting so stressed about difficulties or obstacles in the road. You'll find a greater sense of direction in life and make smoother progress, without so much effort. You'll be able to speak up for yourself, as well as for others, and act as an agent of change, making the world a better place.

Important note: After using any of these Simple Remedies or Full Prescriptions, don't cling tightly to what you *think* the results should be. When you're back in alignment with the natural flow, your life will rearrange itself in ways that may surprise you! But if you're focused on what you think *should* happen, you may not notice the doors that are opening to you. Trust the process and welcome what comes.

Chapter 9

FIRE ELEMENT AND SYMPTOMS OF FIRE IMBALANCES— LACK OF JOY, REJECTION, TRAUMA, AND HEALTH ISSUES

Let's recall the characteristics of Fire Element: it's when energy is at its peak, such as the prime of life when we're at our physical best; summer when all of nature is at full growth; and noon, when the sun is at its highest point in the day.

The Fire stage in human life is when we've completed our physical maturing and are at full vitality. It's usually when we leave home for the first time, thrilled we're finally free to live our own life! It's also when we're more likely to make careless choices, such as in romance, out of excited infatuation.

In summer, we see Fire in the long hours of sunshine, the extra light and warmth stimulating our energy and giving us more time for fun. We tend to socialize more in the summer and care less about responsibilities because we want to take advantage of the good weather.

And we can recognize Fire in how we are at midday, having built up some speed during the morning, so by noon we usually have a lot of projects going at once. This is also the time we tend to break for lunch, often eating with other people in a restaurant, or in a busy office, not in peace and quiet but in a stimulating environment.

We can look to nature as well to understand the feeling of Fire. A flame flickers; it's always moving, never still. Fire can flare up and expand into a wildfire, or it can slowly settle into peaceful glowing embers. But it's also quite vulnerable; a single breath can extinguish a candle flame.

In Chinese medicine, Fire Element relates to our emotional heart, which is the source of our capacity for joy and gives us a natural ability to make others feel loved. It enables us to freely express ourselves without fear of rejection, and to take a psychic "read" on people so we can know whether to trust them with our heart. Our Fire lets us maintain a positive outlook even in difficult times so we're able to live in a state of wonder and delight at the miracle of being alive. And most important of all, this Element gives us the power to always feel lovable within ourselves.

If Fire is not a major part of your personality, there's greater potential for it to dim, because it just won't draw your attention the way the other Elements do. Energy follows attention, after all, so you'll need to remember to give it regular care. For example, Ravi had a lot of Wood Element in her nature, with the classic Wood problem of being too driven. She not only was intensely focused on work, but she'd piled on night classes to her schedule as well, so all she did was go to work, go to class, and collapse into bed. Soon, even on weekends, she couldn't relax and just have a little fun, and it wasn't long until her family started complaining that she was bringing everyone down. This workaholic attitude was certainly counter to Fire's lighthearted approach, so over time, her light started to fade.

If, however, you do feel you have a lot of Fire, the risk here may be that your feelings are so close to the surface, and so easily felt and expressed. This is a wonderful quality, which will cause people to respond positively to you because you're emotionally available to them. But as with any Element, it can also become too much of an influence. Rebecca was an extreme example, an emotionally reactive Fire person who constantly rode a roller coaster of her feelings. She took everything people said to her personally and was always getting her feelings hurt as a result. Most Fire people aren't that out of balance, but if you relate to Fire, notice how often you may feel vulnerable emotionally, or get hurt by someone's words, even though, rationally, you realize that wasn't their intention.

So whether Fire is your main Element or if it's the least present in your design, if it falls out of harmony, there will be problems. Let's discover three common issues that imbalances in Fire create, and then learn remedies that can help solve them.

THREE COMMON SYMPTOMS OF FIRE IMBALANCE

1. Lack of Joy

The emotion associated with Fire is joy, which is not the same as happiness or contentment. It's the exuberant feeling you get when your heart sings, when a flash of pure delight surges through your body and makes your eyes sparkle. It's the exhilaration you feel when you first fall in love, or when it's finally summer and you can go outside in your bare feet. Joy happens in those fleeting moments where you feel connected to the miracle of being alive.

The most pervasive Fire problem in our culture is "lack of joy." We're surrounded by people whose eyes have no light in them at all, because, for example, they're stuck in a job they don't like, or in a relationship where the love is long gone. In our culture, we're conditioned to listen to our heads and not our hearts, so when we're at a crossroads, we choose the path that promises the most money or is most practical in some other way, even though if we paid attention, we'd hear a thud in our heart. And then all that extra money we're earning is spent on doctors' and therapists' bills, because we've lost our joy.

If Fire Is Not Your Strongest Element

There will naturally be times in life when we lose touch with our joy, whether or not we're Fire people. We have losses, heartbreaks, disappointments, and downturns that make our spirit falter and our light dim. Carrie got promoted at work, but one jealous woman spread vicious gossip about her that other people believed. Every day she saw them looking at her and felt their silent judgment. When her boss moved her to a different position with less power, Carrie was sure it was due to this gossip, and felt totally betrayed, by her boss, by that woman, and by the coworkers she'd trusted as friends. She said, "I've shut my heart to the lot of them." But our capacity for joy lives in our heart, so when she shut her heart, she closed herself off from her joy as well and lost her previous enthusiasm for her work.

If You Are a Fire Element Type

It's terrible for anyone to lose touch with joy, but for a Fire person, it's far more significant because joy is the basis for how they need to function in life. Shawna was a Fire woman whose boyfriend shattered her heart when he broke up with her. She was in such pain, she rarely left her house for days because all she did was cry. Eventually the tears stopped, but she was lost in such sadness that she stayed isolated, gradually became morose and lacked the energy to try to pick up the pieces of her life again. For Fire people, healing the heart is a two-phase process. At first, it's right to withdraw and be alone, to let that vulnerable flame gently recover. But the second stage needs to come soon into the process: reentering the world and finding a way to let your light shine again.

2. Rejection

Fire's greatest fear is of rejection, a terribly painful experience for that Element because it means someone would not let you into their heart; in other words, they didn't love you back. Fire's purpose in life is to create heart connections, to make everyone you meet feel special and lovable, and for them to treat you the same way. And the most important function of the heart is for you to be able to feel lovable within yourself. So if someone rejects you, all that goes down the drain and your Fire can go into distress.

If Fire Is Not Your Strongest Element

If you're not Fire, you can still experience rejection, of course, and that can send this Element out of balance. We've already seen in Carrie's story above how, if someone's heart is hurt, it can shut down. This can happen after experiencing rejection too, but there are other ways the heart can react in that situation. Leah felt she had found her soul mate in Krista, and was walking on air for the first three months they were dating. When Krista found out her job was being transferred to another state, Leah exclaimed, "I'll go with you and we can start a whole new life together!" But Krista's response was that maybe this was a good time to just let the relationship come to its natural end. It so crushed Leah that she started a series of short-term superficial flings, chasing anyone to try to regain that feeling.

If You Are a Fire Element Type

If you're a Fire person, you live so much in your heart that rejection is like a direct hit, far more painful than for other kinds of people. You may not think of yourself as fearful of rejection, but instead call yourself shy; however, with Fire people, shyness can always be traced to a fear of rejection. Lucinda was a Fire woman and a very knowledgeable real estate agent but painfully shy, and she had trouble finding clients because of this. One effective way agents find new clients is through holding open houses, but she was so afraid people would reject her that she couldn't bring herself to do this. Instead, she always asked an assistant to handle things, and hoped perhaps someone would pick up her business card and call her. But because they didn't meet her in person, no one did.

3. Trauma

In Chinese medicine, trauma is defined as a "shock" to the heart (Fire), which is considered the seat of consciousness in the body. In other words, when something terrible happens to you, it puts your entire system into shock. Some examples of trauma are having an accident, receiving devastating news, being attacked or abused, or experiencing a major betrayal. This can cause some degree of PTSD, which is the equivalent of what's called "shock" in Chinese medicine. You don't have to be a soldier coming back from war to have PTSD, and even a mild version can be very difficult to recover from.

If Fire Is Not Your Strongest Element

Everyone has some Fire in their nature, and it's what will be most impacted by a traumatic experience. Zoe got a concussion in a car accident and experienced health issues afterward, including headaches and dizziness. Furthermore, her emotions were all over the place, she suffered from insomnia, and she was unable to concentrate—all signs of Fire shock. Chinese medicine teaches that the heart has two functions. One is to flare up in excitement, to feel the thrill of joy and expand it out into the world, like fireworks. The second is for the heart energy to return home to itself and settle, to become peaceful and calm, like glowing embers. When there is a shock to our heart, it can get stuck in an overstimulated state and lose its ability to achieve calm. Then our emotions become erratic, or we're unable to focus our attention or attain peaceful sleep.

If You Are a Fire Element Type

Fire people have open hearts and a beautiful emotional sensitivity. But every personal trait has a downside, and here it's not just that this makes them emotionally vulnerable. Remember that Chinese medicine teaches that our consciousness resides in our hearts, not our brains. So an open heart also means an open consciousness, sometimes too much so. A Fire person may be an emotional empath, someone who soaks in and experiences the feelings of other people. Rowan was a Fire child with an extremely volatile father who had frequent meltdowns where he shrieked and wailed and pounded the walls. She was terrorized by experiencing the intensity of his emotions, and because her mother was too passive to make him stop, Rowan was traumatized again and again. This created a mild but constant undercurrent of PTSD in her adult life that made her highly anxious and never able to relax.

Just as when there is a serious imbalance such as physical or mental illness, if you have had trauma in your life, you should consult someone who's professionally qualified to help your heart and mind find peace again. The Five-Element suggestions in this book can be used in conjunction with treatment and can beautifully enhance it. (Also see the Recommended Resources section.)

HEALTH ISSUES COMMONLY ASSOCIATED WITH A FIRE DISHARMONY

Each of the Five Elements relates to certain organs and functions of the physical system. If there is a health issue with any in the following list, this *might* indicate an imbalance with Fire Element. You should always work with your medical practitioner regarding physical health concerns, and you could easily integrate some of the suggestions in this book as part of your treatment plan.

- Heart (e.g., heart disease, palpitations)
- Small intestine
- Nervous system
- Insomnia
- Rashes (e.g., rosacea, hives)
- Speech (e.g., stuttering)
- Brain function (e.g., concussion, fainting, epilepsy, stroke)
- Memory problems (e.g., dementia, short-term memory issues)
- Tongue
- Panic attacks
- Attention disorders (e.g., attention deficit disorder)
- PTSD

I often see these health issues in people who have a lot of Fire in their personality patterns, but they can be present in anyone's life. We all have some Fire in our makeup and so need to keep it healthy. Fire Element problems of any sort are telling us this energy needs some loving attention.

OTHER POSSIBLE SYMPTOMS OF FIRE DISHARMONY

The examples described above are the problems I most frequently see associated with a Fire Element imbalance, but there are many kinds of issues that can reveal a disharmony in Fire. Some others are:

- Extreme shyness
- Fear of intimacy
- Perspiration problems
- Unstable emotions
- Fame- or attention-seeking
- Some forms of sexual addiction
- Jealousy or gossiping
- Narcissism
- Poor judgment in love
- Scattered thinking or mental confusion
- Manipulative tendencies
- Irrational beliefs
- Vanity
- Inappropriate laughter
- Overstimulated by technology
- Fickleness
- Flamboyance

Chapter 10

SIMPLE REMEDIES AND FULL PRESCRIPTION FOR FIRE ELEMENT

We'll start by discovering choices for Simple Remedies for Fire Element problems that you recognize are just affecting you temporarily. Then in the next section you'll find a Full Prescription that gives you the steps to follow instead, if you know that a Fire issue is more constant or recurrent in your life.

SIMPLE REMEDIES

Remember you have five options for how to bring Fire back into balance because each of these five energies offers help in a unique way. Four of the choices come through the Nourishing and Control Cycles, and the fifth comes from enhancing Fire itself.

You can try any or all of these remedies listed below, but not at the same time. Choose one to start and give it a chance to work for several days. Although they may seem inconsequential, remember they are the equivalent of acupuncture needles stimulating points of energy in your life, and so can create powerful shifts for you. Our inclination is to think that only actions that require big effort are effective, but that's actually not how any change in this world occurs!

1. Enhance Fire:
Speed Up—Fast-Paced and Fun Exercise

Fire energy is stimulating, fast-paced, and fun, so here, you could choose exercises that match that vibration. For instance, sign up for Zumba, salsa, or tap-dancing classes, or work out to fast music. And amazingly, just jumping up and down in place can be effective. Even if you're feeling that your Fire is overstimulated and unsettled, this can be a remedy, because "fighting Fire with Fire" has the remarkable effect of calming the system down. In other words, stimulating an already overstimulated system can actually burn off the excess energy.

Jason was an author who had to give a series of public lectures, but he suffered from terrible stage fright, which is a Fire issue. Right before he went on, his anxiety would flare up, his heart would leap into his throat, and he thought he might pass out. One day he spontaneously started jumping up and down backstage and was astonished to find that he quickly felt calmer. He went out and gave the best of all his talks and got a standing ovation at the end!

2. Drain Fire with Earth:
Find "Mother" Energy—Seek Out a Grounded Friend

Sometimes Fire just needs help to remember its job is to move toward Earth; in other words, to settle and get grounded. One way to do this is to connect with someone you consider solid, sensible, and kind—in other words, an Earth personality. This could be a trusted family member, a close friend, or a therapist, but it could also be someone who's like a mother figure to you, such as an older woman you feel comfortable with.

Elizabeth's new job was at a large corporation and she struggled to learn the ropes with all the different departments and managers. Her ambition was to rise up the ranks as fast as she could, but her Fire was making her seek attention in all the wrong ways, and one day, she was horrified to hear colleagues gossiping about how she always tried to grab the spotlight (which is a Fire Element issue). She approached a manager who was an older, maternal type, and asked her to mentor her—just what the doctor would have ordered to calm down her Fire—and the rumors stopped.

3. Focus Fire on Metal:
Appreciate—Experience More Beauty in Your Life

This remedy helps Fire remember that one of its jobs is to control Metal. One aspect of Metal Element is experiencing and appreciating beauty, so if you add more beauty to your life right now, you'll be strengthening Metal, and as a result, Fire can perk up and return to healthy movement.

There are so many ways you could incorporate more beauty in your daily life. You don't have to purchase an expensive piece of art! It can be as simple as noticing a lovely scene on your commute to work. When Connor felt his Fire was all over the place, he quickly made a list of what he could do in one week: visit his city's art museum, create a centerpiece for his dining room table, play his favorite classical music as he worked, buy the silk shirt he'd been lusting after, or spend an afternoon at the arboretum to take in the beauty of nature all around. This was a bit of a Firey approach! But it worked all the same: his Fire rebalanced after its attention was directed to Metal.

4. Control Fire with Water:
Hydrate—Drink Water and Eat More Soup

Another choice to return your Fire to health is to bring in its controlling Element, Water. One easy way to add Water to your life is to literally add water! Stay well hydrated by drinking plenty of water and other healthy liquids throughout the day. But the very best way is to include more soup in your meals, because it has the natural minerals and salts that correspond directly to Water energy. It can be any kind of soup, though bone broth is excellent because bones relate to Water Element, or soup with fish, seaweed, or seafood, since they're sourced from the water!

Lianna's fast-paced lifestyle always had her rushing, arriving late, and forgetting things. She long ago gave up on carrying her water bottle with her because she constantly lost it, and she mostly just drank coffee all day. After increasing her water intake and having a few dinners with a big bowl of soup, she said she felt the difference viscerally. "I hadn't realized how scattered my energy was, and this is starting to make me feel cohesive again."

5. Nourish Fire with Wood:
Schedule Sleep—Be in Bed before 11 P.M.

Chinese medicine has found that at 11 P.M., Wood Element moves into a very important phase in your biorhythms, and if you go to sleep before that time, it keeps this energy healthy. If you stay up late, the opposite happens: Wood is weakened and then won't be able to support Fire as it should.

But May couldn't get to sleep at 11 P.M. because of her insomnia, a common sign of a Fire imbalance, and the usual advice to have a totally silent bedroom didn't help at all. In fact, if Fire is causing insomnia, it's actually better to listen to a podcast at bedtime, and she found it immediately worked for her when nothing else had. This is another example of "fighting Fire with Fire," in other words, adding some stimulation calms the overstimulated energy. However, don't leave the television on; the flickering light is not good for this Element. Music, calming sounds, or meditations won't be effective; it has to be the sound of people talking. But even if you don't have an issue with insomnia, going to bed by this hour can help heal a problem caused by a Fire imbalance.

FULL FIVE-ELEMENT PRESCRIPTION TO REMEDY LONG-STANDING FIRE ELEMENT ISSUES

When Fire Element isn't just causing a temporary issue in your life, but instead, you recognize it's been a theme in your problems for years, then you should use a more complete Full Prescription that you follow for one full month, just as if this was doctor's orders. For example, if people have often told you that you take things too personally, or if you've experienced many heartbreaks or betrayals, this suggests Fire probably has been in distress for quite some time.

Remember, this is not a lifelong prescription; it's meant to be followed every day for one month. Select as many of the following choices as you like, but remember that you don't have to do all of them. These are the equivalent of acupuncture needles applied on a whole-life scale, and can create powerful shifts for you. Begin with three or four of them and you can add or change to others if you like. However, don't select any that go against your own tastes or that conflict with your doctor's advice.

Add Fire to Your Wardrobe

Red is the main color associated with Fire, but other options are bright orange, hot pink, rich purple, or any very bright, vivid color. So one idea would be to wear more of any of those shades, as long as you like how you look in them. You don't have to dress entirely in any of them; you can wear them as a part of your total outfit.

Animal prints or sparkly jewelry would also qualify, and since Fire is about passion as well, you might wear clothes that make you feel luscious and sexy! These don't have to be visible to the outside world, because this is about how *you* feel, not how you're trying to make others feel, so even sexy lingerie that no one else sees would be a Fire cure.

Fire type shoes have pointed toes and/or spike heels. Changing your hair color to red, or the style to a spikey or curly cut, or a shaved head would also add Fire to your life!

Create a Firey Environment

You could add any of those Fire colors to the décor of your home and office too, with little touches here and there so you can always see one wherever you are. Art that promotes this energy could include those Fire hues, or any shapes that are peaked or pointed, or images of the sun or hearts. Hanging crystals or prisms in the windows to sparkle or act as rainbow makers would add Fire to the room, or just turn on more lights to make your environment more bright and cheerful. Flowers are Fire energy, so bringing in flowers from the garden or the store would be a good choice now. And adding actual fire such as burning candles or having a fire in the fireplace would certainly qualify.

Fire is also about playfulness, so displaying quirky or fun objects, or anything humorous would work as well. Lastly, images of birds or recordings of their songs would bring Fire to your surroundings, as they have a strong relation to this energy in Chinese medicine.

Do Fire Activities

Spend Time with Fire

One option is to literally spend more time around Fire. So aside from lighting candles or a fire in the fireplace as mentioned above, a backyard barbecue, or a bonfire on the beach would qualify, or simply cooking more meals on your stove rather than in the oven or microwave. (It doesn't matter whether the stove is gas or electric.) And since the sun is definitely "fire," spending more time out in the sunshine is another choice.

Have Fun

Fire activities are any that make you light up, that you love to do even if they seem like a silly waste of your valuable time! If your Fire is in need of boosting, it's possible that it may be hard for you to remember what "fun" even is because it's been so long.

This doesn't have to be a big production—remember, these are supposed to be small actions. Take a few minutes to play with your pet each day or goof around with your kids, for example. Or hang out with the person you always end up in a gigglefest with. If you were forced to take an afternoon off with the stipulation that you could only spend that time on something fun and unproductive, what idea would leap into your mind? Escape from your normal life for at least two hours and do it.

Even when you're not able to take off to do something fun, look for ways you can make whatever it is you're doing more fun. When you clean the house, turn the music up loud and dance as you go!

Exercise

Workouts that match this Element are anything fast-paced, such as salsa dancing, Zumba, or tap dancing. Try something that's done in a fun social setting, such as an exercise class where you laugh and chat with others rather than doing it alone.

Socialize

Fire is about a heart connection, as well as stimulation. You can get both by socializing with people you like. Go to parties or throw one of your own, but only if you'll be with people you truly enjoy. Invite a friend to a live performance such as a play or a concert, or to visit a gallery to view original art, because these carry the live qi of the artist, which excites the heart in ways copies don't. Take a few minutes to chat and joke with colleagues rather than keeping your nose in your work all day. Smile and start a cheerful conversation with the person next to you in the checkout line at the store and brighten their day!

Be Seen

If we remember that this Element has to do with the sun at its peak, illuminating everything, then we can understand why Fire is like putting you in the spotlight, making you visible. So one way you could put this to use is to find ways to be "seen." You might volunteer to teach a course, make a presentation at work, or perform in a local theater production. You could make silly videos, even just for your family and friends, or post more photos of yourself on social media. Create time with someone you love who you feel will really pay attention, and talk about yourself, your feelings, or what you're going through right now, in a way that will make you feel truly seen as a person.

Express Yourself

Fire relates to communicating, so look for every opportunity to do so, especially if it can be a heart-to-heart conversation. Confide in a friend over coffee, call someone you love, or have more special moments at bedtime with your child where you tell them how much you adore them.

Fire is also expressing yourself creatively, whether that's writing, dancing, or cooking—anything that feels creative will do. And you might want to think about what message you want to communicate with your creation as well, because this can be a way to share what's in your heart with the world.

Lift Your Heart

This Element is what makes you feel lit up, and in its highest form, is a sense of enlightenment. So to align with that energy, you might listen to inspirational audios, go to lectures or classes about spirituality, watch movies or read books that speak to your soul, or practice forms of meditation that lift your heart and leave you feeling illuminated.

Engage Your Sense of Wonder

What are you fascinated by, or what makes you feel a sense of wonder and delight? For some people, it's travel, where you see amazing sights, meet interesting people, and have an escape from your humdrum everyday life. So you might schedule a trip to someplace you've never been before, whether it's a weekend out of town, or an adventure to an entirely different part of the world. Or instead of travel, you could visit a planetarium to experience the awe of seeing the stars and the vast universe, or a botanical garden, full of exotic plants and blooming flowers. Think of what would make you say, "*Oh!*" and do that!

Hand Out Compliments

This Element gives us the capacity to make others light up, and it's the energy that causes us to feel joy in doing so, thus feeding our own Fire too. Every chance you get as you go through your day, hand out compliments like they were candy! Praise a colleague's work, exclaim to a friend that you love the color of their shirt, tell the store clerk how efficient they are, and watch the light in their eyes change. And it's likely that sometimes you'll get a compliment back, and your assignment in that case is to accept, not to say some version of "Oh, this old thing?" but to brightly respond, with something like "Why, thank you!"

Kindle Your Passion

Add more passion to your life to help your Fire recover. If it's been so long since you felt passionate, you may need to reach back in time to remember what used to make you feel that way, and that's okay. And it doesn't have to be something that anyone else would find special, so don't be shy. Some people may swoon at an excuse to read romance novels, while others may lust after shopping for shoes. It doesn't matter what the activity is; it's about how it makes you feel. And you can take passion literally, of course—having great sex qualifies too!

Align with the Magic Hours for Fire

As we've learned, in each 24-hour period, our systems progress through different phases of the Elements, and if we align our activities with the one in power at each stage, we'll more easily stay in balance. Fire is strongest from 11 A.M. until 3 P.M.

This is a time that's most supportive of Fire activities, and when you can benefit from this Element's influence. Fire is stimulating and quick energy, so you can use these hours to your advantage by working on any projects that require you to have plenty of energy and a sharp mind. Having lunch with friends is also a Firey activity, so choose that more often instead of eating alone.

If you notice you feel keyed up or overstimulated at midday, or alternatively, if you feel drained and tired, this probably indicates that your Fire is out of harmony, and you definitely need to attend to it!

Increase Fire Element Foods in Your Diet

Have fun with food! Make an entire meal of hors d'oeuvres, or eat dessert first and soup last. Make sure there's a lot of variety in your meals and include lots of brightly colored vegetables on your plate. Prefer cooked meals over cold ones and try new recipes or visit restaurants that you've never been to before, especially if they offer different cuisine than you're used to. Dark green, bitter-tasting vegetables like kale, arugula, or spinach are good to add to your diet, preferably cooked instead of raw.

Fire Practice: Lovability

In order for your Fire Element to stay in balance, you need to be able to decide which people are deserving to open your heart to, so that you can trust that the love you express will be accepted and honored, not rejected or abused. But even more importantly, you must be able to know, in your heart of hearts, that you are lovable. You need to love yourself.

One exercise you might try to increase the love you feel for yourself would be Louise Hay's mirror work. This is a practice where you look at your reflection in the mirror and try saying, "I love you. I really, really love you!" Or if that's too difficult, you can start with "I like you," or "I really want to learn to love you." You may feel silly at first, or you may be surprised at how emotional you get doing this practice, but if you keep at it, the results can be powerful ones. (See the Recommended Resources for more information about Louise's mirror work.)

You might do any of the wonderful "loving-kindness" meditations that brilliant Buddhist teachers such as Sharon Salzberg and Jack Kornfield offer, or any other heart-based meditation practices. And keep the love flowing with little acts in your daily life, because the more outward expressions you make of this energy, the more it fills your inner spirit as well. Pay attention to even momentary feelings of warmth and affection, and expand them throughout your body. You might spend more time with animals or babies, who can be much easier to practice love with than some adult humans!

Ask your friends and family to take a few minutes and make a list of what they like about you—don't be shy! You may be astonished at all the nice things they say. And sit down and make a list of what you like about yourself too. Recognize that despite any limitations or difficulties, you're always doing the best you know how to do and striving to stay in your heart, and that's a totally lovable quality.

Fire allows you to let someone into your heart and form a deep intimate connection. This takes a willingness to be open and vulnerable, but also to have the discernment to know whether that person can be trusted to enter your most private territory. Your heart must not be so desperate for love that it lets someone in if they're not able to love you in healthy ways.

Chinese medicine refers to "discernment" as the function that allows you to gauge whether a person is safe to welcome into your heart, at what rate, and how fully. The organ called the Heart Protector, which is equivalent to the pericardium, the lining of the heart, acts as the Guardian of the Gate of your heart. Imagine that your doorbell rings and you peek out to see your best friend standing there. You'd fling the door wide open, give them a big hug, and bring them into your home, wouldn't you? If it's an acquaintance, you might invite them into your living room, but not farther into the house. And if you see a total stranger standing there, you might open the door a crack, or not even open it at all and just speak to them through the door. This is an example of the Heart Protector's function, and the kind of discernment you need to use to keep your heart safe. Don't let someone into your heart until you get to know them well enough, and as you do, take care with how quickly and deeply you allow them in at each step of the way, because it'll be at a different rate for each person.

In any interaction, practice being aware of how you feel around that person, and notice how that can change during the course of your conversation, depending on their behavior or what they say. You'll be growing your ability to take a "psychic read" on someone as well as manage the boundaries of your heart in healthier ways. Keeping your Heart Protector in balance will help you attract relationships with people who are emotionally available to give you love in the ways you need.

As your Fire Element heals, you're better able to follow your heart as well as your head, listening to what it whispers to you, even if it doesn't always make logical sense, and thus more easily stay on your path in life. You'll reclaim your sense of joy, each day full of fascination and delight. In difficult times, you're never down for long, always able to see the bright side and regain a positive outlook. You'll be able to form close relationships with people who return your feelings in healthy ways. You'll beam love toward everyone you meet, and when you look in the mirror, you'll feel totally, endlessly, profoundly lovable.

Important note: After using any of these Simple Remedies or Full Prescriptions, don't cling tightly to what you *think* the results should be. When you're back in alignment with the natural flow, your life will rearrange itself in ways that may surprise you! But if you're focused on what you think *should* happen, you may not notice the doors that are opening to you. Trust the process and welcome what comes.

Chapter 11

EARTH ELEMENT AND SYMPTOMS OF EARTH IMBALANCES— WORRY, WEAK BOUND- ARIES, LACK OF SUPPORT, AND HEALTH ISSUES

Let's go over what we know about Earth Element: It's the phase in the cycle when the energy starts to settle and solidify. In middle age, we begin to slow down physically; historically, in early fall, the harvest was in and there was abundant food for everyone; and in early afternoon, most of us have full stomachs and hope we can just sit and not work so hard for the rest of the day.

The Earth phase in life comes after we've reached our peak physically, and it's when many people start to get a little thick in the middle. This is also a time when we don't feel as driven in life. We've reached a certain level in our career, or have family and its associated responsibilities, or been able to afford a nice home, that we want to take more time to enjoy.

In early fall, our attention begins to focus more on our responsi- bilities instead of summer fun. We tend to family needs as the kids go back to school, and we may also start to feel drawn to accumulating some new knowledge ourselves. Autumn is often when adults take classes or put their noses back into personal growth books rather than the novels they read on the beach!

And in the early afternoon, when we're usually full from lunch, we start to slow down. It can be hard to be as active as we were in the first part of the day, and we just want to sit and work more quietly.

We can understand this Element by thinking about how it is in nature too. Earth is quite literally terra firma, settled and solid. And in Chinese medicine, it relates to mother energy, grounded and calm. Mother's job is to nurture her children so they will thrive in life. It's the same as the rich soil nourishing the crops so they'll grow healthy and strong.

Our very first relationship in life is with our mother, and she is really the one who teaches us the language of relationships. So it's our Earth Element that gives us a natural kindness and generosity and empowers us to have a healthy give-and-take with others, where we happily step up to be there for the people we care about, but are also receptive to their support in return. The same energy allows us to feel fulfilled by our work, and to experience regular moments of contentment as we go through each day. This Element helps us feel centered and secure so we can put down roots in a home we love, and develop lifelong friendships with people who feel like family to us. Most importantly, healthy Earth enables us to be as nurturing and compassionate toward ourselves as we are toward others.

Even if you know you don't have much Earth in your personality, it's still part of who you are, and so needs to be cared for. And as we know, when an Element isn't a major aspect of someone's design, the risk is that they can disregard it too easily. For example, Amos was a Wood person who gave more time and energy to his work than his relationships, which is not uncommon for people of this type. But he rarely allowed himself even the small Earth action of pausing to feel a moment of satisfaction during the day when one task was completed before moving on to the next on his list. All his Wood controlled his Earth so much, Earth went out of balance, and one of the results was a lack of support when he needed it, both personally and professionally.

If you do see that Earth is a major factor in your design, then it may be in the driver's seat too often. For instance, because you're so innately other-directed, you can be too much of a "giver," and wear yourself out helping people, or not have time to take care of your *own* needs. Most Earth people consistently neglect their self-care, not always in obvious ways, but with small subtle choices as they go through their day. It will just seem right to them to put others first and sacrifice their own needs, just as a mother does for her family. Earth woman Deborah, a social worker, was amazed to realize how guilty she felt just thinking about leaving work an hour early after a nonstop stressful week taking care of all her clients without a moment to herself.

Earth Element is an important ingredient in your personal recipe and needs be kept in the right kind of balance. If not, problems will start to form, and over time can affect all the Elements in the circle. Let's examine three common ways this can happen with Earth imbalances, and then see how we can use the Five-Element cycle to solve them.

THREE COMMON SYMPTOMS OF EARTH IMBALANCE

1. Worry

The emotion associated with Earth in Chinese medicine is most easily translated as "worry." The best way to understand this Element is as mother energy, and one thing we know about mothers in every culture is that they constantly worry about their children! But Earth people not only worry about their children; on an unconscious level, they feel a motherly responsibility toward everyone in their lives, and that's a lot worrying to do! Because energy follows thought, every time you worry about someone, you send some energy their way. So you can get worn out by all the worrying you do, even if you're not running around taking care of others.

But another translation for how Earth people's minds function is "rumination." One definition for the word *ruminate* is "to chew over and over." When worries go around and around in your head, it's as if you are chewing your thoughts without digesting them. In Chinese medicine, Earth Element relates to digestion, and when thoughts go undigested, they interfere with your ability to think clearly, just like undigested food in the gut causes blocks or stagnation.

If Earth Is Not Your Strongest Element

If you don't relate much to this energy, you can still get stuck in worry at times, of course. Worry is not the same as overthinking, however, and one way to differentiate it is that worry is emotionally based, and often involves thoughts about others, or our responsibilities toward them. For instance, Brad was offered a job that he'd really enjoy but which would involve uprooting his family from the town they loved, plus his children would have to leave all their friends and start a new school in the middle of the year. So he really struggled with the decision, feeling guilty about putting his needs ahead of his family's, going around and around in his head about whether it was worth the stress it'd cause them. The more he worried, the less clarity he had, and in the end the job offer was withdrawn because they could no longer wait for him to decide.

If You Are an Earth Element Type

If you're Earth, you may already recognize yourself as a "worrier"! But you may not notice ways this tendency can cause problems beyond just the stress of worrying. For example, Lilly always felt it necessary to explain the entire history of a problem, how everyone involved felt about it, what each person said and what she said back, and then what *they* said, etc.! Earth people are storytellers, and with her mother energy, it was natural for her to worry about everyone's needs being considered. But going around and around this way often made her lose focus on the subject at hand, or ended up confusing the person she was speaking to. And if that happened to be a Wood person, they'd quickly become impatient with her and say some version of "Get to the point! What's the problem and how do we fix it?!"

2. Weak Boundaries

A mother is always on call; she's never off duty. If her child cries out for her in the middle of the night, she never says, "I'll be available again at 8 A.M.!" She immediately goes to them; she'd feel unbearable guilt at the thought of letting her child stay in distress. While this is an appropriate response for a mother toward her child, what can happen with our Earth is that we behave this way outside of a mother-child relationship, meaning that we don't always set healthy boundaries, whether within our family or outside of it. For example, with weak boundaries, you might do too much for family, friends, coworkers, and clients, or simply have trouble ending a phone call with an overly chatty person. You might have a hard time saying no, or let people take advantage of your kindness, or frequently end up working late because you've taken on—or been given—too many responsibilities.

If Earth Is Not Your Strongest Element

While you may not have much of this energy in your personal patterns, if your Earth goes out of balance, it can influence you to make poor decisions about boundaries in your life. In that case, you may be surprised that it's hard to limit what someone can ask of you, or how much effort you invest in a project. Rhonda was so eager to prove herself in her new job, she came in early, stayed late, and volunteered for projects no one else wanted to do. When her supervisor asked if she'd be willing to take on some extra tasks, she immediately said yes, and soon found herself burdened with far more than any human could do in normal working hours. She'd lost her boundaries and now worried if she scaled back, she'd lose ground at work and get a bad performance review.

If You Are an Earth Element Type

Earth people frequently don't think to define the terms of an agreement; in other words, set the boundaries. When Tiana learned her friend Jasmine signed up for a three-month training in her city, she immediately said, "I've got a spare bedroom, so you can stay with me! If you can just contribute to my rent, that'd be great." Jasmine eagerly agreed. But Tiana hadn't defined the terms of the agreement. Her rent was $2,000 a month, but when Jasmine moved in, she only contributed $50. The three months passed, and though her training was over, Jasmine showed no signs of going home! Tiana felt terribly guilty at the thought of asking her outright to leave, so she stalled for weeks, until she got so angry, she exploded, and that was the end of their friendship. If she'd set some boundaries at the beginning, all this could have been avoided.

3. Lack of Support

In nature, the role of a mother is to support her children, but it's not their job to support her. A mother's first thought is some version of *How can I help you; what do you need; have you eaten?* It'd be a foreign experience for her to think any other way. As well, children naturally look to their mother for support rather than considering what *she* needs. This is just how it's meant to work—mother takes care of her child, but the child doesn't take care of her. If your Earth is out of balance, this scenario may play out in your personal and/or professional experiences. In other words, you may repeatedly feel like you're always there for people, but that you don't get the support you need from others. For example, when you ask for help from friends, they're unavailable even though you've done so much for them. Or perhaps they do show up but don't give anywhere near the amount of assistance you need. These can all be signs of an Earth imbalance.

If Earth Is Not Your Strongest Element

Even if you know you're not an Earthy type, this Element can still fall out of balance and result in a lack of support. For instance, Matthew was a Water person who was very quiet, as most Water types are, and he also carried that Element's belief that he was an outsider and that no one would include him as part of their group, so he never really tried to engage with others. As a result, he didn't have a community of friends he could ask for support when he needed a ride to the airport or was looking for a new job. If you recall, Earth is the Element that controls Water. Here, Water was already quite a strong influence, and as Matthew continued to not pay enough attention to Earth (relationships), that Element fell out of harmony and thus was less able to function in healthy ways.

If You Are an Earth Element Type

If you're an Earth person, you may be thinking, *Huh, a lack of support is the story of my life!* When you have a mother personality, people sometimes feel they really can't help you, because they see you as already totally capable on your own. But Earth people also can lack receptivity, and so may not even recognize when support is offered, or turn it down when someone says, "What can I do?" Andrea was over her head preparing for a big family reunion and really needed help with all the errands. But she didn't want to impose on her relatives because "they're all so busy." And she rationalized that even if she did delegate some of the chores, they wouldn't be done right anyhow, so she'd be better off just doing them herself in the first place. Earth people need to be aware of how they may contribute to a lack of support from others.

HEALTH ISSUES COMMONLY ASSOCIATED WITH AN EARTH DISHARMONY

Earth Element relates to specific organs and functions of the physical system, so if there is a health issue with any in the following list, this *might* indicate an imbalance with Earth. You should always consult your medical practitioner about physical health concerns, and you could easily include some of the suggestions in this book as part of your treatment plan.

- Stomach (e.g., digestive problems)
- Spleen and pancreas
- Overeating, or craving starches or sweets
- Frequent bruising, or cuts and bruises slow to heal
- Diabetes, or blood sugar problems
- Breasts (e.g., breast cancer)

- Muscles (e.g., poor muscle tone)
- Flesh (i.e., the area between the skin and bone)
- Mouth, lips, gums
- Congestion, mucus, sinuses
- Brain fog
- Fibromyalgia
- Chronic fatigue

I've frequently seen health issues with these aspects of the body in people who have a lot of Earth in their personality patterns, but I also see them in people who have little of this Element in their nature. This is because they can easily forget to nurture their Earth, so it becomes weakened. However, *anyone* can develop Earth issues, of course, no matter what their main Element is. We all have some Earth in our design, and we need to keep it in the right balance for us. Earth problems are telling us it needs some care.

OTHER POSSIBLE SYMPTOMS OF EARTH DISHARMONY

The three examples described above are problems I frequently see associated with an Earth Element imbalance, but there are many others that can reveal an Earth issue. For example:

- Codependent
- Neglectful of self-care
- Lack of confidence
- Self-sacrificing
- Feeling stuck in life
- Meddlesome
- Passive or overly dependent
- Victim mentality or martyr complex
- Bitterness or resentment
- Passive-aggressive

- Overgiving
- Selfish or needy
- Excessive complaining
- Lack of receptivity
- Certain types of hoarding
- Inability to put down roots
- Difficult relationship with mother in childhood

Chapter 12

SIMPLE REMEDIES AND FULL PRESCRIPTION FOR EARTH ELEMENT

When you encounter a problem associated with Earth that you see is new and not long-standing, a Simple Remedy approach can nip it in the bud and bring balance back in short order! So first we'll look at ways to solve temporary Earth issues, and then we'll discover a Full Prescription, to approach problems that have been part of your life for a longer time.

SIMPLE REMEDIES

In every case, we have five options to choose from because each of the Elements can provide its own unique healing effect. Any of the choices below can work for you, but that doesn't mean you need to do them all. Just one can be enough, but if you want to do more, or all of them, that's fine too. Just give any you choose several days to process and take effect. Don't take a scattershot approach to rebalancing!

1. Enhance Earth:
Self-Care—"Re-mother" Yourself

These days, when we talk about self-care, we usually mean eating healthy food and getting enough sleep and exercise. But that's not how self-care is defined in this case. It's being as sweet, kind, and nurturing to yourself as a mother would be to her beloved child. So the best way to think of self-care here is as "re-mothering" yourself, doing little kindnesses for yourself throughout each day, and making sure your needs are well met.

You may have to firmly tell yourself it's not selfish to take time to enjoy life for once rather than always tending to your vast list of chores! Remember this is medicine for your spirit, and of course, if you don't take good care of yourself, you can't be there to care for others as you want to. Amelia had to force herself at first, buying herself a treat at coffee break, getting a quality carry-out dinner so she didn't have to cook or clean, and then curling up afterward to finally read the novel she'd bought months ago. But after adding this behavior over five days, she was shocked that people were calling her out of the blue to offer a hand with a difficult project she'd been struggling to find help with.

2. Drain Earth with Metal:
Clean—Clear Clutter and Add Beauty

Earth feeds Metal, so giving attention to Metal can return Earth to its natural movement. Metal is about purity, simplicity, and beauty, and one way to do this is by cleaning your house, but with a certain emphasis. It shouldn't be about rooting through your closets! Instead, use a two-step process to make your *visible* surroundings look and feel more beautiful. First, put away projects sitting on tabletops, clear the counters in the kitchen and bathrooms so they feel more empty and spacious, and eliminate any other visual clutter. If you don't have the time or energy to do this throughout the house, then focus on the one or two rooms you spend the most time in.

The second step is to add beauty, which can be as simple as a single flower on your desk, or rearranging the throw pillows on the couch. What you're aiming for is that the moment you enter the room, you automatically take a nice deep breath because it looks and feels beautiful. Faith tried this process with just her living room and bedroom, and felt it had a direct impact on all the worries that had built up in her life recently; suddenly things seemed simpler to figure out.

3. Send Earth to Control Water:
Immerse Yourself in Water—Take a Soak!

Because it's Earth's nature to want to control Water Element, it's always important to have enough Water energy in your life, to keep your Earth in active health. One way to do this is to actually place yourself in water! For the next several days, take a bath each evening, or soak in the hot tub, or go swimming—whatever's most appealing to you. Taking a shower is not in this category because it's not the same as immersion, and it's too quick an experience.

After Emily moved to the other side of the country from her family, she made very few friends, despite trying to meet people of like minds. She really wanted to find her people, but so far, nothing had worked. Her condo unit didn't have a bathtub, but there was a community pool a short distance away, so she decided to choose this remedy and started going there to swim. On her fourth visit, she happened to meet two women who soon became fast friends with her. She hadn't intended to go to the pool to make friends, just for a swim, but in doing so, the Elements had worked their magic!

4. Control Earth with Wood:
A New Plan—Create a Structured Schedule

Here, we can use Wood's linear, structured mind-set to bring balance back to Earth. Are there defined times each day when you have client appointments or pick up the kids, but is most of the rest of the day left blank on your calendar? This doesn't mean free time, of course; it's usually a holding area for all the dozens of things you need to somehow fit in! To use this remedy, create a more structured daily schedule. You might identify the tasks that you tend to do at certain times and put them in those spots in your calendar. Then look at the others on your to-do list and try to assign them a specific time as well. If something happens that day to interfere with the plan, you can simply adjust and reassign that chore to another spot or another day.

When Miguel tried this, his original calendar was mostly blank, but this in no way represented how busy and productive he was! He just never assigned things to particular times in his schedule. As he created more of a structure to each day, he felt more in control than he had before, when all the Earthy responsibilities just seemed to spread through all his waking hours.

5. Nourish Earth with Fire: Express Your Creativity—Play and Experiment

Fire is about expressing yourself creatively, so even if you don't think you have an artistic bone in your body, free yourself to play around, to experiment for once, because Fire is also about having fun with a project! You can choose anything: compose a song, or make a collage, for instance, as long as you feel free to do what strikes your fancy.

Grace was a single mother of two and felt like she was on a treadmill in life, running as hard as she could, with never any time off. She said, "I keep calling out to God to send me help, but nothing ever comes." One day as she watched her daughter play with watercolors, she decided to plunge in and join her. She painted a bright sunrise with birds swooping through the sky and it made her so happy, she joined her daughter in creating another picture the next day and the day after that. "I started to wake up to the fact that I could just enjoy my life with my kids the way it is right now instead of feeling like I had to struggle so hard." Her Earth was becoming healthy again.

FULL FIVE-ELEMENT PRESCRIPTION TO REMEDY LONG-STANDING EARTH ISSUES

When a problem associated with Earth has been present in your life for a long time, it's better to use this deeper approach that you carry out for one full month. Start out by choosing three or four of the suggestions below, and then you can add in more or change to different ones over the course of the month. As always, don't select any that clash with your own tastes or go against what your doctor says. What's most important is that you do at least one of these every day for the month, without skipping days.

Add Earth to Your Wardrobe

The main color associated with Earth Element is yellow, but these also qualify: beige, brown, gold, soft pink, peach, or warm pastels. So one choice would be to wear more of these colors each day. If you love earth tones, then don't hold back, but if you don't like them, simply add them in small touches, such as carrying a brown tote bag or wearing a beige shirt.

Or you could choose to dress in a more Earthy way, with comfortable clothes as a priority, especially nothing tight around the waist. If you have to dress up for your job, then the first thing to do when you get home is to change into your sweats or pajamas! Earth types of shoes are flat with rounded toes, so even your feet are as comfy as possible.

Create an Earth Environment

Those Earth colors can be incorporated into the décor of your home as well, such as a yellow quilt on the bed, or a brown rug at the front entry. You might add artwork with those colors, or other choices would be images of landscapes, mountains, pastures or farms; or of food, like a still life of fruit in a bowl. Pictures of groups of people, such as family photos, also match this energy.

Earth has to do with receptivity, so including "receptacles" in your surroundings would be another option, such as baskets or bowls. But because Earth is about abundance and feeling full, you might fill the receptacles with something, like a collection of pretty rocks or seashells in a basket, for instance.

Aim for a sense of coziness and comfort in your environment. Choose to sit in the big overstuffed chair or cushy couch rather than on a hard chair, and make sure your desk chair is supportive and the desk itself feels solid and substantial. Clear any projects off the dining room table so you can use it for meals and actually try to eat together as a family more often than not.

Do Earth Activities

Gather

Earth energy is a gathering force, so any kind of activity where people come together would be a fit here. You might have more outings together as a family, or visits with friends. Go to a lecture, a workshop, or a party, or invite people to your home for a meal, or to work together on some mutual interest, or organize a family reunion. Any opportunity to join with others can be a form of Earthy gathering.

Collecting things is a form of gathering as well, so you might start a collection or add to an existing one by shopping, or going to garage sales or secondhand stores. Buying groceries and restocking your pantry is another form of gathering, and directly relates to Earth since this Element has to do with nourishment.

Exercise

An Earth workout is when you exercise with at least one other person, so long as it's easy and enjoyable, with more emphasis on the togetherness than exercise! For example, take a walk or a bike ride with a friend, or participate in exercise classes, if the teacher is not an unsympathetic drill sergeant type, and avoid any classes that are advertised as "bootcamps"!

Eat

While Earth is directly associated with being nourished, this is not an invitation to eat unhealthy food or snack mindlessly while you watch TV! This is an assignment to cook more often; even making some simple meals can do wonders for boosting this Element. Or when that's not possible, try to choose "homemade" food from restaurants; in other words, consciously cooked by a person, not something that was microwaved or sat under a heat lamp and then was thrown in a container.

Help

Because this is mother energy, we look to what a mother does to find ways to add more Earth to our lives. Mother's first thought is always some version of *What do you need—how can I help you?* So, this month, look for ways you can help others. Lend a hand whenever you spot someone in need, be more generous with your time or energy at work, watch for little ways you can care for family and friends, or do some volunteer work.

However, if you're a woman, it's very possible you're already overloaded with time and effort spent helping others, so you may be thinking, *This is the last thing I need!* What you can try instead, then, is not to add more of these kinds of activities but to reframe your experience whenever you do help someone. It's possible that all this helping has come to feel like just part of your daily grind, and it can weigh on you a bit, as yet another demand on your limited supply of time and energy. Can you pause a moment and experience some sense of satisfaction at having helped someone? A mother loves to take care of her family; it makes her feel fulfilled. Try to move into more of that feeling each time you assist another person and then those actions become more of a benefit than a detriment to your energy.

Be Receptive

Earth Element also means receptivity, like a mother opening her arms to her child, to gather them into her lap, or letting someone you love embrace you in a warm hug. In this case, your job is to find little ways in your daily life you can be more receptive to help. Observe yourself: Are there moments when someone offers to lend a hand that you turn down, saying, "Thanks, but I've got this"? Your thought process may be that it's just easier to do it yourself, but over time, that can lock you into a subtle belief that you have to do everything yourself, and this diminishes your receptivity in all other aspects of life. So try to say yes more often to offers of help. Let the employee at the store load the groceries into your car, allow a friend to buy you lunch, or lend a hand with a chore. Soften toward offers of help and your Earth will start to transform.

Practice Self-Care

These days, the concept of self-care is mostly a bunch of *shoulds*! We *should* exercise every day, *should* get to bed earlier, and on and on. But this makes life even more full of responsibilities! Here, self-care takes on an entirely different meaning. Again, think of the stereotypical mother caring for a child. You could think of her work as a bunch of *shoulds*, but that's not her attitude at all. Instead, she naturally treats her child with kindness and generosity. It makes her happy to do special things for her child, to make them feel loved and safe in her care.

Here, the practice of self-care is mothering *yourself* in that way. As you go through your day, look for opportunities to be kind to yourself. For example, buy yourself a special treat, or curl up to read that book you've been saving, or take time off for a stroll in a beautiful setting. Put something nice you'll do for yourself at the top of your to-do list every day, and don't sacrifice it, no matter what. And how kind are you being to yourself with the thoughts in your head? You'd probably never speak to anyone else as critically or negatively as you do to yourself. As often as you can, try to shift your internal dialogue to one this is more compassionate and accepting.

Create Clutter

There's so much guilt about clutter in our culture today, so you may be surprised I'm not only *not* going to nag you to clear it, I'm actually going to ask you to create a version of what you might think of as clutter! As you look around your house, it's likely that here and there, you'll spot little objects that you've accumulated over the years that carry some sentimental value for you. These could be mementos from trips you've taken, or gifts people have given you, or things you've collected that you just like the look of. The only requirement is that just the sight of them brings back happy memories or puts you in a good mood.

Put these on display—arrange them on the mantle or a tabletop, or prominently on a shelf. It's best to group them together rather than spreading them throughout the house, because you want to create a sense of fullness, not sprawl. And if there's any clutter nearby, move it away or get it organized so that when you pass by, you're not distracted; your attention goes right to a sight that immediately makes you feel good.

Ground Yourself

We're talking about the "earth" after all, so another option would be to get outside and touch the earth! Walk barefoot on the ground or sit on the grass, if the season permits. Or go for a stroll in a park, or on the beach, or out in the country—anyplace where you're not walking on paved surfaces but instead on the grass, sand, or soil. Do some gardening if it's the right time of year, or get some potting soil and make a nice new home for your indoor plants. (I do not recommend purchasing any contraptions that promise to "ground" your energy, as I've consistently found these actually have an adverse effect on your system and your environment.)

Set an Intention

While imbalanced Earth can make someone ruminate, or worry, the balanced form of this energy can be described as "intention." The best way to understand its meaning is to think of what Mother does at the start of her day. She thinks carefully about everything she has to accomplish: her projects at the office, running errands for the family, making sure she has dinner figured out in advance, etc. She always has a lot on her plate, so she has to be thoughtful in her approach to each day so nothing falls through the cracks. Earth Element is about completion, bringing things to fruition, and "intention" is the process of making sure that happens.

At the start of each day, rather than hit the ground running, take some time to pause and think in an intentional way about what you need to get done. Though this may result in a to-do list, it's not the same thing as Wood-like goal-setting or creating a regimented schedule. Instead it's a more grounded, thoughtful approach that helps create a calm, cohesive energy to your day.

Align with the Magic Hours for Earth

The most powerful time of day for this Element is between the hours of 7 and 9 A.M. This time frame is also most supportive of the digestive process, but not only in terms of your stomach. It also relates to the digestion of thoughts in your mind.

Chinese medicine teaches that if you're not digesting food in your stomach some time during this two-hour phase, you won't be able to digest your thoughts. In other words, you won't plan your day well and then you won't complete tasks that are important, not only for the day, but also for the long run in terms of your dreams and goals. Even Western medicine has recently discovered there is a direct connection between the gut and the brain.

So, eat breakfast between 7 and 9 A.M., and you'll be able to think things through and thus complete the work you need to that day. (Avoid cold smoothies, however, as pouring cold liquid into the hot digestive juices actually stops digestion. If digestion is halted in the stomach, it stops in the mind too.)

Increase Earth Element Foods in Your Diet

To help your Earth, add more root vegetables to your diet, especially any that are yellow or orange, like sweet potatoes, winter squash, and carrots. Beans, seeds, and nuts help this energy, as do vegetables that grow in tight layers, such as onions, cabbages, and artichokes. Meals should be cooked and eaten warm, and drinks should be not be cold. Avoid dairy and sugar, but don't deprive yourself of treats or your favorite comfort foods now and then. And enjoy what you eat!

Earth Practice: Cultivate Contentment

The concept of "mother" in the spiritual teachings of Chinese medicine has many layers of messages that can help you understand how to keep your Earth energy in balance. One of the most important is the need to regularly experience a feeling of contentment, which is not the same as happiness or gratitude. Contentment is a feeling of calm satisfaction and fulfillment. Picture the archetypal mother sitting in a rocking chair, smiling as she gazes down at the baby sleeping peacefully in her arms. All is well in her world; she has everything she needs.

Contentment is when we feel "full." It can come at the end of a wonderful meal, when we push back from the table with a nice sigh of satisfaction. It's how we feel after a job that's been well done and we pause to let that sense of completion really soak in. A nature image for Earth is the parched soil soaking in fresh raindrops, which conveys that "Ahhh" feeling of being nourished. Earth is about bringing something to fruition, which in real-life terms, has to do with getting what you need, feeling "well fed" in every way.

So the practice here is to consciously cultivate more contentment in your daily life, and there are many simple ways to do this. Sitting is Earth behavior, so be sure to sit down at the table for your meals instead of eating on the run, and most importantly eat until you're *full*. I don't mean feeling uncomfortably stuffed, but don't push away from the table early! You're aiming for that sense of satisfaction you get when you have a meal that was just what you needed.

Take at least a few minutes every day to sit and enjoy your home. Choose the comfiest spot and settle in; then look around the room. What little things do you see among your belongings that warm your spirit? Perhaps it's simply how much you like the colors in the rug on the floor, or a souvenir from your travels that brings back good memories. Notice all the possessions you love, and really let those nice feelings fill you up.

Contentment can also be cultivated by cuddling your pet or child, or giving/receiving hugs from friends and family. And as you work each day, practice pausing for a few moments after you finish each task and allow yourself a sense of satisfaction that it's *done* before you move on to the next thing. Let that soak in just like the raindrops soaking into the ground.

As your Earth Element heals, you develop better boundaries, because you're taking as good care of your own needs as you are everyone else's. With your growing ability to be patient and thoughtful, life starts to feel more stable overall. You gain more of a sense of belonging with family, or with people who feel like family to you, and you find you're happier with where you're living. Your work will become more fulfilling, and as you transform to become more centered and grounded, you discover you're more supported in life, as if there's a mother tending to your every need.

Important note: After using any of these Simple Remedies or Full Prescriptions, don't cling tightly to what you *think* the results should be. When you're back in alignment with the natural flow, your life will rearrange itself in ways that may surprise you! But if you're focused on what you think *should* happen, you may not notice the doors that are opening to you. Trust the process and welcome what comes.

Chapter 13

METAL ELEMENT AND SYMPTOMS OF METAL IMBALANCES— ANXIETY, LACK OF SELF-ESTEEM, MONEY ISSUES, AND HEALTH ISSUES

Now we arrive at our final Element, Metal! Let's recall what we know about it: this phase of the cycle relates to old age, the last stage of life; and the time the year draws to a close; as well as evening, the final part of the day.

In old age, we are increasingly aware that our lives are coming to an end, and so we often reflect on the past with a mixture of both regret and gratitude. We also look ahead and may feel some anguish about not enough time left to us, or anxiety about whether there are enough savings to see us through.

Metal is represented by the season of late fall, when life in nature also seems to be coming to an end, and historically, this was a time when people concentrated on making sure there was enough food to last the winter. They knew scarcity was coming in that season, and so were careful not to waste anything.

Additionally, this Element relates to early evening or the end of the day, when we're clearing our desk, preparing to finish our work and go home to rest. We try not to leave our workspace a cluttered mess, but to clean it up as much as possible so we can take a sigh of relief as we depart.

In nature, Metal as a substance is valuable ore like gold and silver, and it also relates to rocks and crystals, which are hard and inflexible. But in Chinese medicine, this Element also has to do with the concept of "heaven" and the sky, drawing our eyes upward, to inspire us to aim high in life. And Metal is the archetype of "father" as well. Traditionally, the father is the authority in the family, the one the children look up to and want to make proud. (Even Western psychology often teaches that the one thing any child craves is for their father to be proud of them.)

Metal inspires us to live authentically, aligned with our highest principles, so we can feel a genuine pride in who we are and who we're becoming. It gives us a sense of the sacred, reminding us of what's most valuable to focus on so we don't waste our time on trivial endeavors. This is the Element that empowers us to discover our true purpose in life, and to do meaningful work that fulfills that calling. And Metal allows us to transform our losses, regrets, and griefs into wisdom and gratitude, like the final stage in the alchemical process of turning lead into gold.

Whether or not you related strongly to the description of a Metal personality, there is still some of this energy in your makeup, and so it needs to be cared for. It can require more effort to remember your Metal when it's not a major part of your nature, because you'll just automatically see life through the filter of your more dominant Elements, and this can cause problems. For example, Teri was an Earth woman who struggled with self-esteem issues. Earth energy often gives people a very sweet humility, but if it becomes too much of an influence, they're unable to feel genuine pride in their accomplishments or let others give them credit when they merit it. Teri constantly shrugged off praise from her boss at work, and as a result, he lost respect for her and didn't offer her a promotion she deserved.

If you do have a lot of this Element, it creates a filter that can distort your view and limit your possibilities. Metal's movement is to contract and tighten, and one result can be that a Metal person gets very uptight about things. William was house-hunting but was highly anxious about little aspects of each property. When he found a house he liked, he parked in front of it at different times of day and night so he could monitor the noise level in the neighborhood. He insisted on finding out the kind of paint used on the walls and which sealant had been put on the wood floors. He researched the history of property values in the neighborhood, agonizing over the prospect of buying the house and then having it lose value. Because he spent so much time on this hyperanalysis, other buyers took house after house before he could decide.

Even if Metal is not a significant influence in your personality, it's still a part of your makeup. If there's an imbalance in its energy, it can cause problems in any or all aspects of your life. Let's look at three issues that I often see come up with a Metal disharmony, and then go on to discover ways to remedy them.

THREE COMMON SYMPTOMS OF METAL IMBALANCE

1. Anxiety

Metal governs the grief process, the journey through loss, guiding us until we can begin to see glimmers of how what we've been through has actually enriched our lives, and then we can begin to have a growing sense of gratitude, even within the grief. Metal gives us the power to make meaning out of loss, to find value in the experience, to make gold from lead.

In our culture, the word "grief" tends to be defined too narrowly; we usually relate it to what we feel when someone has died, or when a love relationship is lost. But the emotion of grief actually has a much wider reach in our lives. It has to do with how we deal with any kind of loss, anticipating even the possibility of a loss, and even with feeling lacking as a person. In fact, while struggles with grief are definitely Metal issues, the emotion of *anxiety* more accurately describes the many subtle ways we experience this energy's influence on a daily basis. For example, anxiety comes as a response to feeling that things may not work out as we need them to (because we'd react by grieving that loss). Or we can be anxious that we might make a mistake, or that we aren't good enough as we are (both forms of loss or lacking).

If Metal Is Not Your Strongest Element

Whether or not you have much Metal in your nature, you can still experience anxiety, of course, although it won't be like the constant undercurrent many Metal people experience. Something may happen that triggers an anxiety about not being good enough or fear of failure. My client Biyu made a big mistake in a contract with her company's most important customer, and the resulting pandemonium sent her spiraling into anxiety about the quality of her work. She began to wonder if she was even up to this job, and became obsessed with rechecking each new contract multiple times and procrastinated about every decision, feeling she had to get it absolutely right. She developed insomnia, waking up with a start every hour or two, anxious that she still might have overlooked some little detail and that she was about to lose her job.

If You Are a Metal Element Type

If you're Metal, you probably experience anxiety on a daily basis, or you don't even know what it feels like to *not* be anxious. As one of my clients said, "It's my normal!" Metal people are often hypervigilant, their system always on high alert. Other times, Metal anxiety can show in an inability to let go, even when there is no value in holding on. Charlotte wanted to get married and have children, but her boyfriend had no interest in being a father, or even in a commitment. He dated other women and only saw her every few weeks. She knew she should let him go but said, "What if this is the best I can get? What if I let him go but then can never find anyone else?" Her Metal anxiety about lack kept her stuck in a situation that actually guaranteed lack.

2. Low Self-Esteem

Low self-esteem also comes from a sense of Metal lack, or what I call "enough issues." This is a condition where we feel that we're lacking, not good enough in some way: not attractive enough, successful enough, intelligent enough; we didn't do something well enough; or we *might* not do something well enough, so we don't even try! We may not even be aware of how frequently our self-criticism affects us in subtle but pervasive ways. An anxiety about being lacking can actually create a life of lack because it makes us limit our choices, keep our life too small, and be afraid to take a risk, because if we fail, our inner critic will become unbearably loud.

If Metal Is Not Your Strongest Element

If your main personality isn't Metal, poor self-esteem may not be on the top of your list of personal challenges, but there can still be phases in life when your pride takes a hit. It could be an experience where you feel you're not getting the respect you deserve, or you may compare your progress to a colleague's big success and start to feel that you should have achieved more by now. Anthony grew up with a highly critical father, and he'd internalized that voice as his own inner critic. Even after doing years of personal work to lessen its influence, there were still times when it controlled him. When the sports team he managed had a spate of bad luck, he started to notice that disapproving voice getting louder, trying to convince him the team was failing because he wasn't good enough.

If You Are a Metal Element Type

For a Metal person, low self-esteem can cause frequent anguish throughout their life. Perfectionism could make them cringe at the tiniest of mistakes, and keep that "not good enough" program running in their minds. Natalie told a group of friends she was researching an article about weight loss, and they all compared notes about the various diets they'd tried. Because her friend Marta was the most enthusiastic, Natalie asked her if she could interview her for the article. Marta's smile vanished and she changed the subject. Later Natalie received a furious email from her, accusing Natalie of purposely trying to embarrass her and call her fat in front of everyone. While any other type of person would know this was ridiculous, Natalie took it to heart, horrified to think she'd unconsciously been so mean, and agonized for months about it, her self-esteem hitting a new low.

3. Money Issues

Any imbalanced Element can create problems with money for different reasons, but Metal has the greatest potential to cause *emotional* issues around money, which then affect its energetic flow into or out of your life. The Metal belief pattern of "not enough" could make someone pinch every penny and live in deprivation because they're so anxious about finances. At the other extreme, Metal's desire for the very best and to feel proud can cause them to overspend to get the highest quality of everything, and to impress other people. And in the middle of the range, any financial lack might reveal a Metal imbalance, often due to not feeling deserving of "enough."

If Metal Is Not Your Strongest Element

If you're not a Metal person, there can still be times when your approach to money is influenced by this Element's energy. For example, my client Beth's self-esteem was at its lowest point after five years as a stay-at-home mom in an emotionally abusive marriage. While she was finally able to get a divorce, she applied only for low-paying jobs, because she felt she wasn't worth more. Carlos, another client, was burdened with such huge debt from student loans that he plunged into extreme Metal anxiety about money. As a result, he cut way back on his spending, buying only thrift-store clothes and selling his car. While it can be good to live minimally, he went too far, and these choices affected his ability to get a job because he needed a car and a professional wardrobe. The negative influence of unhealthy Metal can cause someone to choose a life of deprivation.

If You Are a Metal Element Type

If you recognize Metal as part of your design, you may already know that at times, concerns about "enough" money can be too great an influence on your decisions. Or you may have always dealt with anxiety about finances, even if rationally, you could see you have enough and probably always will. It's not uncommon for a Metal person to look at the amount of income or savings they have and feel overwhelmed that it's not enough, while any other person looking at that same amount would feel secure. Cathy was a Metal woman who refused to marry her lifetime partner because she couldn't bear the thought of having to be financially affected by his choices. Even though he wasn't careless with money, and his additional income would actually make her safer financially, she couldn't get past her irrational concerns.

HEALTH ISSUES COMMONLY ASSOCIATED WITH A METAL DISHARMONY

Each of the Five Elements relates to certain organs and functions of the physical system. If there is a health issue with any in the following list, this *might* indicate an imbalance with Metal Element. You should always consult your medical practitioner about physical health concerns, and you could easily integrate some of the suggestions in this book as part of your treatment plan.

- Lungs (e.g., asthma, bronchitis, lung cancer)
- Large intestine (colon) (e.g., constipation, irritable bowel syndrome, Crohn's disease)
- Skin (e.g., psoriasis, eczema, vitiligo)
- Depleted immune system
- Allergies
- Environmental sensitivities
- Dryness (e.g., hair or skin)
- Nose or sense of smell
- Autoimmune illnesses

- Hypersensitive nervous system
- Anorexia
- Obsessive compulsive disorder (OCD)

As we know, health issues associated with an Element are often found in people whose personalities carry the same energy, but anyone can develop issues related to any Element, no matter what their personality patterns are. We all have some Metal in our makeup, and so need to keep it in the right balance for us. Metal Element problems are telling us this energy needs some loving attention.

OTHER POSSIBLE SYMPTOMS OF METAL DISHARMONY

The examples described above are the problems I most frequently see associated with a Metal Element imbalance, but there are many kinds of issues that can reveal a Metal issue. Here are some examples of others:

- Perfectionistic; self-critical
- Aloof and distant
- Self-righteousness; dogmatic
- Extremely minimalistic or materialistic lifestyle
- Difficulty with intimacy
- Self-conscious
- Overly critical and sensitive to criticism
- Controlling, bossy
- Stuck in the past, lost in regret
- Arrogant or conceited
- Self-deprivation or overindulgence
- Difficult relationship with father in childhood
- Certain types of hoarding
- Rigid, uncompromising
- Unresolved grief
- Sense of entitlement, demanding
- Overconcerned with cleanliness

Chapter 14

SIMPLE REMEDIES AND FULL PRESCRIPTION FOR METAL ELEMENT

If you have a new problem that relates to Metal Element, then a Simple Remedy may bring balance back to resolve it. However, if this is an issue you've struggled with for years, it may be better to use the Full Prescription that follows this section.

You can choose any of the Simple Remedies listed below, or you can even go through them all if you'd like. But with any that you try, do one for at least several days, so it has time to process and take effect before you try another. You may have to remind yourself that, though these actions may seem illogical to the "rational" side of your brain, there actually is a scientific foundation for their effectiveness. The reason you swallow a pill your doctor prescribes is because you long ago accepted the concept that it'll affect how your body functions. Here, we're expanding our understanding, so we can accept that a small action will affect how your life functions.

SIMPLE REMEDIES

1. Enhance Metal:
Establish a Rhythm—Make Life More Predictable

Because Metal is the energy that makes you highly aware of all the details in any situation, it naturally lends itself to anxiety because there are so many things to keep track of! So the fewer specifics you have to scan for, the less vigilant you'll have to be. Metal benefits from a sense of regular rhythm and predictability in life, because the more you can anticipate what's going to happen, the less you have to stay on top of.

Look for little adjustments you can make in your everyday life to create a more predictable rhythm. For example, this week, you might get up, go to sleep, and eat each meal at the same times each day. Organize your clothes for the next day the night before so you don't have that extra bit of stress in the morning. Charles precooked the entire week's dinners, separating them into individual frozen meals so each night there would be no thought needed. He was amazed, not only at how soothing it was to come home and just pop one in the oven, but also at the effect it seemed to have on reducing his anxiety in other ways as well.

2. Drain Metal with Water:
Get Messy—Create but Don't Control

One Water "cure" is to do something creative, but you'll have to be careful that you don't just bring a Metal approach to what should be a Water activity! In other words, avoid letting your Metal fuss with every detail, or strive to get the project exactly right. Instead the way to do this should be exploratory, not trying to control the outcome, but just letting go and seeing what magic can happen.

So, for example, rather than painting a picture with fine brush strokes, throw out the brush and try finger painting! That can be especially challenging for a Metal person because it involves getting goo directly on their fingers and making a mess, which they have a natural aversion to, but this is exactly the kind of thing that can help their Metal let go. Whether you're a Metal person or not, the final step in this process is not to get upset if you feel your creation isn't any good. Sharon got creative in the kitchen, ignoring any recipes, and experimented with different ingredients and techniques. There were hits and misses, like the cookies that spread into shapeless blobs, but she was able to disregard the failures and found this effect rippled into her life to help her relax more overall.

3. Direct Metal toward Wood:
Pick a Spot—Clear Clutter and Get Organized

Adding Wood to your life can help Metal come back into balance as well. Metal is most affected by visual clutter and isn't so bothered if there's a mess hidden behind closet doors or inside drawers. But with this remedy, we don't want to aim for a space that just looks beautiful on the surface. We're taking a Wood approach here, which is about getting organized so your life works more efficiently.

However, this isn't an assignment to declutter your entire house! Remember, these are the equivalent of acupuncture needles, stimulating *small* points of energy, which can then get a big response. So just choose one part of your home to clean and organize. It can be as simple as your kitchen junk drawer, or as ambitious as your entire closet. Toss out what you don't need and then organize the rest so the space works more efficiently for you. When Jessie's self-esteem was at rock bottom, she went through her pantry, which was so jammed with supplies, she no longer even knew what was there. After she created a new system on the shelves, she said, "I was surprised to feel such a sense of pride!" That small act was like vitamins for her Metal.

4. Control Metal with Fire:
Light Up—Add Actual Fire to Your Life

One easy way to increase Fire energy in your life is to literally add real fire! Burn candles, and use the fireplace if the season permits, or play a video of a crackling fire on your TV. Use the stove, even if that's just to boil water for tea or reheat leftovers. (It doesn't matter if the stove is gas or electric.) Go to a firework show or look online for images from Fourth of July or New Year's celebrations. Have a barbecue or use your backyard fire pit if you have one. And if there's a restaurant in your town where meals are cooked at tableside, that would qualify as well.

After losing his job, Josh developed such severe distress about money that he couldn't even bring himself to look at his bank statements. He went into immediate overwhelm if there was a problem with a bill, and procrastinated dealing with it. And when tax time rolled around, he was terrified that he'd not have the right records to complete the paperwork for his accountant. Suspending his skepticism about this simple remedy, he diligently added fire to his life, and after 10 days, found himself spontaneously pulling up his bank records online, something he hadn't been able to do for months!

5. Nourish Metal with Earth:
Help Out—Volunteer in a Group Setting

Here, we can use two aspects of Earth: gathering and helping. Look for an opportunity to volunteer in your community, as long as it's done in a group setting. It's even better if you do something Earthy, such as an activity to do with food, shelter, or families, for instance. So don't take on a solitary activity like making phone calls from home, but perhaps lend a hand at the local food bank, or work on a team building a house for Habitat for Humanity. The point is that you do the equivalent of mother energy by helping others without getting paid, and that you do it in a group setting, like a mother with her family.

Christina wanted to join an online dating site but felt anxious that her photo wasn't attractive enough, so she kept procrastinating. She couldn't imagine something so insignificant as volunteering would have any effect on those feelings, but she gave it a try, helping at a homeless shelter in her town. She had expected to have to repeat this for several weeks before she noticed any results but was mystified that even after her first time there, her level of anxiety lessened enough that she chose a photo for her dating profile and posted it.

FULL FIVE-ELEMENT PRESCRIPTION TO SOLVE LONG-STANDING METAL PROBLEMS

If you believe Metal has been causing more long-standing problems in your life, then instead of choosing a Simple Remedy solution, you should work on a Full Prescription that you carry out each day for one month.

Any of the choices below can help you. Start out by using at least three or four of them, and you can add in more if you like, or select different ones as time goes on. Just be sure to do at least one of them every day without fail. If any of these recommendations go against your personal tastes, or are what your doctor said to avoid, then don't include them.

Add Metal to Your Wardrobe

The main colors associated with Metal Element are white, gray, and metallics like gold and silver. So one choice here would be to wear more of these colors over the next month. Remember you can add them in small touches if you like, such as a gold necklace or a white shirt.

Metal clothes are ones that feel good on your skin, so for instance, avoid scratchy fabrics and remove bothersome labels that rub against your neck. Metal fashion is very refined and minimalistic, often with calm, monochromatic colors or classic designs. Metal styles of shoes never have rounded or squared toes, and even athletic shoes need to look elegant! And because this Element is about authenticity and quality, if you own real pearls, gemstones, or polished stones, choose to wear those rather than costume jewelry.

Create a Metal Environment

You can also use those Metal colors in your surroundings in subtle ways, such as white napkins, or a gold vase on a table. To add artwork that carries Metal energy, aside from these colors, you could choose scenes that have an expansive view, far into the distance, especially if the outlook is from a high place, such as a picture of the landscape seen from a hillside. Images of the sky and clouds also qualify, especially if they have an inspirational feel to them.

Metal is the influence that makes you most affected by visual clutter, not the stuff that's hidden away in closets, so here your focus would be on what's visible! Clean off surfaces and simplify what's out on display. If you have a wall full of pictures, consider how you might hone it down to a bare minimum or even just one perfect image! All this will reduce the overstimulation of having too many things calling your attention when you enter a room, which will stress your Metal. Aim to create an environment that when you walk into a room, you feel a sense of spaciousness and calm.

Do Metal Activities

Choose Predictability

Look at what you can to do create a regular, predictable rhythm in your day. For example, maintain set times for bedtime, waking, and meals that are the same every day. Figure out tomorrow's outfit the night before, and place everything you need to take with you in the morning by the door. Plan your weekend in advance so you know what's coming. Of course, circumstances can intervene and that's okay. This is not meant to force you into a regimented schedule, but actually to relax more into knowing that what can be under your control, is!

Get Subtle Energy Work

Metal is the most subtle and etheric of all the Elements, so any kind of subtle energy work would be good for you at this point. Examples are treatments like acupuncture, flower essences, essential oils, somatic therapeutic work, or energy clearing. Avoid more forceful treatments like Rolfing or intense chiropractic manipulations during this time period.

Spend Time in Wide Open Spaces

Metal equates to air and the sky, and so conveys a sense of spaciousness. To align with that energy, go somewhere that has that feel to it, especially if it's up high. You might gaze out a window in a tall building, for example, or just spend time outdoors in a spot that has an expansive view of the sky. You could visit a place that has large open rooms, like a museum, or you could even just view pictures of clouds and sky on the internet.

Keep an Appreciation Journal

Keeping a gratitude journal is one way of stimulating your Metal, but I find that approaching it that way often comes with a sense of obligation, like you're *supposed* to be grateful, and that feels a bit heavy. Instead we can remember that Metal is about appreciation, like in old age, when we revere each moment as precious, because we know it may not come again.

So here, you'd keep an *appreciation* journal, noting special moments you experience during your day. For example, you could write about how fresh the morning air smelled, or the lovely patterns the shadows and sunlight made on your wall. Record how delicious your latte was, or the love that welled up in your heart as your dog greeted you at the door. What you may find is that you soon start carrying this journal with you all the time because you're constantly observing things that you treasure!

Create a Sacred Space

Designate a room or area of your house as "sacred space" to use only for special purposes. It could simply be a chair that you sit in to meditate, read inspirational books, or write in your journal, but not to pay bills, or make phone calls, for example, or an entire room where you do qi gong, yoga, or spiritual practices.

I'd highly recommend doing a space clearing for your entire home as well, so it'll hold a pristine vibration, to beautifully support your connection with your sacred self. You can use the step-by-step method in my book *Clear Home, Clear Heart: Learn to Clear the Energy of People and Places,* or you could create your own space-clearing cere-mony, perhaps with candles, or sound healing techniques. However, I don't recommend smudging with sage in an attempt to clear the space because at best it only has a superficial effect, and much of the time I find it actually muddies the energy there.

Practice Breathwork

In Chinese medicine, Metal relates to the lungs, and also how the breath is taken in and then let go. When this Element is out of balance, we can breathe too shallowly or even hold our breath without being aware of it. See if you can catch moments in your day when, because you're stressed or anxious, you're not breathing fully enough, and take a nice deep breath. You might consider a breathwork practice for this month, whether that's during a yoga class or studying one of the various forms of breathing exercises that appeals to you.

Exercise

Beauty is the key here, so any graceful form of a workout will fit. Examples are tai chi, qi gong, ballet, or any kind of movement that looks elegant and refined. Metal exercise would not include anything that leaves you dirty or drenched in sweat!

Foster Self-respect

In this practice, you nurture a genuine sense of pride, not of the egotistical kind, but a very authentic respect for who you are and who you're becoming.

First, make a list of what you achieved in the past year, even the things you might think are too inconsequential to be included. For example, you read more books, took a workshop and learned a new skill, were better disciplined about bedtime, saved a bit more money than you thought you could, etc. You may assume you won't come up with much, but once you start thinking back, you could find yourself creating quite a list!

Next, make a new list, this time of past achievements, such as degrees you've earned, and even any minor accomplishments that made you feel proud of yourself at the time. Then add in all your good qualities, personally and professionally. For instance, think of what you've done in each of your relationships (past and present) that made you a good friend, relative, or partner to that person. Write down what you admire about yourself, such as having good taste in clothes, being athletic, or your skill at gardening. List all the ways you're good at your job, even minor details that at first you might not think matter—they do.

<u>Tune into your "body feel"</u>

Metal Element gifts us with a type of intuition in the form of physical sensations that can provide valuable insights and information. For example, practice noticing how you feel around a certain person or in a particular environment. Were you fine until you stood near that person but then once you did, you started feeling tired, or dizzy, or just a bit "off"? Were you feeling one way before you walked into that office, but once you got in the door you became uncomfortable for no obvious reason? These sensations can not only clue you in to what's happening in the energy around you and how you're being affected but can also keep you from thinking something's wrong with you! And if you have a decision to make, go ahead and analyze so your left brain is happy, but after that, tune in with your body. If you feel a physical thud inside, maybe it's not the right decision after all. If you feel your cells light up, then even though it may not be the most logical choice, it could be the way to go. Make use of both your mind and your body to guide you.

Align with the Magic Hours for Metal

Every few hours, we're immersed in the energy of one of the Elements, and if we adjust our behavior to match that influence, then we'll more easily stay in balance in life. The important phase for Metal begins at 3 A.M. and lasts until 7 A.M.

Since we know that Metal is about a sense of the sacred, it's not surprising that in many religious and spiritual traditions, practitioners rise at these very early hours to meditate or pray. You can benefit from this phase by devoting even a few minutes during this time frame to some spiritual practice. Aside from praying or meditating, you might create a simple ritual to greet the day, or even just take a few minutes to breathe quietly and become totally present and aware.

Increase Metal Element Foods in Your Diet

Quality is essential for healthy Metal, so eat organically as much as possible, and choose the highest quality ingredients for your meals. Beauty is another aspect of this Element, so arrange your food artfully on the plate! And why not use the best china, place flowers on the table, and play music to make the experience as lovely as possible?

Foods that relate to Metal have a pungent flavor, such as garlic, onions, mustard, and horseradish, and since the color associated with this Element is white, vegetables like cauliflower, turnips, and parsnips are a match as well. Lastly, if you suspect you have an allergy or even a sensitivity to certain foods, eliminate them from your diet this month. Reintroduce them later, one by one, so you can tell which might cause a reaction when you eat it again.

Metal Practice: Letting Go

Aside from contracting, the second kind of movement for Metal in nature is to let go. In the fall, the trees let go of the leaves; at the end of our day, we stop what we're doing and prepare to sleep; and at the end of life, we may pare down possessions as we move out of our home and into a smaller space. Physically, we're less able, so we have to give up some activities, and overall, we're aware that we're moving closer to letting go of our body entirely.

One of the organs that relates to Metal is the colon, which has an important function in elimination; in other words, letting go. During this process, the colon extracts what's valuable from the waste before it's gone. This applies on a spiritual level as well: Metal is the Element that helps us to gain wisdom *because* of difficult experiences, not despite them. So if we're still in pain from some long-ago experience, or carrying regrets from the past, this is a sign we've not yet been able to "find the treasure in the trash," to recognize the value of what we've gained even as a result of that suffering, and feel gratitude. When we do this, we're finally able to let go of the pain, or put down that burden of regret, and look forward, not back. In this way, we can continue in our personal evolution, enriched, not diminished.

Start out by looking around your house with an eye to what needs to be let go of. In other words, this is not about organizing your belongings but about eliminating some. Go through your bathroom cabinet to see if there are any expired medications that need to be tossed, and look in your refrigerator to find any food that should be thrown out. Identify anything in the house that you're holding on to "just in case" you might need it in the future, even though you haven't used it in ages, and consider getting rid of it. Dispose of any clothes in your closet that you haven't worn for more than a year or that no longer fit.

However, remember these are meant to be small actions, so don't go overboard! On day one, you shouldn't empty your closet and sort through a mountain of clothing! That would be exhausting and too much to do all at once. Just go through one drawer, for instance, and then a few days later, work on another part of your space. Every small "letting go" can create a substantial response from life.

If you come across belongings that, rationally, you know should absolutely be eliminated, but emotionally it's difficult, then honor them in some way before you let them go. It could be as easy as holding each in your hand for a few moments and saying "thank you," or you might even create a ceremony that is meaningful for you. All religious traditions have rituals to deal with loss and grief, and these are the feelings you're experiencing, even though on a very small scale.

But the most important part of this remedy is the final stage— you have to get these things *out* of the house! In other words, don't pile them in a bag by the door, or even in the garage or the trunk of your car, where they're likely to sit for days or weeks. Whatever you're passing on to friends, or any donations for the thrift store, get them there within the next 48 hours, and things that go in the trash should be out of the house that day!

As your Metal Element heals, you're better able to determine what's important in life and let go of the rest. You gain greater clarity about how to live in ways that feel authentic and meaningful to you, and to connect with your sacred sense of purpose. Your awareness heightens so you can appreciate more and more of the beauty around you every day. Your feelings of personal worth increase and you no longer take your self-critical thoughts so seriously. You find you can grieve and move on without holding onto regret, enriched by your experiences, through the alchemy of Metal transforming lead into gold.

Important note: After using any of these Simple Remedies or Full Prescriptions, don't cling tightly to what you *think* the results should be. When you're back in alignment with the natural flow, your life will rearrange itself in ways that may surprise you! But if you're focused on what you think *should* happen, you may not notice the doors that are opening to you. Trust the process and welcome what comes.

PART III

FIVE-WEEK
LIFE REBOOT!

*All living things come out of the mysterious workings
and go back into them again.*

—ZHUANG ZHOU

Chapter 15

WEEK ONE: REPLENISH YOUR WATER ELEMENT

In previous chapters, we've been looking one by one at each Element and ways to remedy its imbalances in order to solve problems in your life. But what if you're not sure which Element to focus on, or you just feel stuck overall in life and can't seem to get things moving again? In cases like these, you can reboot the system: restart the ways your life energy is meant to move, to get it going in the right direction again with an easy, graceful flow!

Each week in the following program gives you certain steps to take, as well as actions to *avoid*, to support one of the Five Elements. Don't skip a week or take a break—and be sure to continue for the full five weeks. It's imperative to do these steps in the order presented. The Elements move clockwise around the circle, beginning with Water and then moving into Wood, Fire, Earth, and finally Metal. This is how the patterns of nature flow, each Element nourishing and strengthening the next one in the cycle, and it's how the qi of your life is meant to flow as well.

This five-week program has been designed so you don't have to even think about the *why*s, *what*s, or *how*s of the Elements. All you have to do is follow the instructions and trust the process. If you find yourself slipping back into a skeptical mind-set, thinking these little actions couldn't possibly affect your life in any meaningful way, remind yourself that just as a few acupuncture needles can shift the qi flow in your entire body to bring your system back into balance, these actions are the equivalent, for your life.

Okay, here we go with your reboot! Read on to find out what to do—and not do—in Week One.

THREE STEPS TO TAKE RIGHT NOW

These are the single most important yet easily achievable actions for this week.

1. Eat more soup.

In Chinese medicine, the energy of soup supports the first level of your journey here. The essential minerals it contains are directly associated with Water Element, and soup also gives you a fantastic boost in hydration, which is important right now too. Any kind of soup is fine, though bone broth or soup with fish, seafood, or seaweed is best of all because they're directly related to the energy of this Element.

2. Take one hour of downtime every day.

What is downtime? Here's what it's NOT:

- Zoning out in front of the TV
- Scrolling through social media
- Spacing out playing computer games
- Catching up with email
- Doing mindless housework

Downtime deeply replenishes our reserves, so we have renewed strength to carry on. It's essential because without a balanced ebb and flow to our days, we get overstressed and start to burn out. But our culture doesn't value downtime. It pushes us to work and get things done; to make money and get ahead. For most people these days, the only downtime they get is through sleep, and the majority of people don't even get enough of that. Another way people try to get it is by mindlessly spacing out with technology, but this doesn't have the same effect, and in fact it is just another subtle stressor on their system. Here are some examples of true downtime:

- A luxurious soak in the tub. (Maybe even add candles and music . . .)
- Daydreaming, gazing out the window, letting your thoughts wander
- Getting a massage or spa treatment
- Meditating or listening to a guided meditation
- Losing yourself in a novel or movie
- Sleeping late and/or lounging in bed for an extra hour
- Anything that makes every cell in your body relax and go "Ahhh."

Choose something from the list above, or come up with your own ideas that match that same feeling. Chinese medicine teaches that the very best part of the day to take downtime is between the hours of 3 and 7 P.M., but if that's not possible for your schedule, *anytime is fine!* The most important part of this practice is that you must have at least 60 uninterrupted, consecutive minutes of downtime each day, not 5 minutes here and there! (And if you can stretch it to more than an hour, even better.) Do not skip a day and try to make it up on the weekend—it's essential to have a full hour or more each of these seven days.

3. Get one hour of dreamtime.

This is different from downtime, but just as important. And unlike getting downtime each day for seven days, dreamtime only needs to be done once this week. (You can do it more than once if you want to.)

In this hour, you're meant to set aside your to-do lists, or any thoughts of planning for the next day/week/month/etc. This time is not to be spent being "productive" in the way we usually think of it. This hour is meant to be more about letting your creativity flow.

For some people, that might literally mean creating art, or writing, or making crafts. But for other people it will be creativity in terms of letting your imagination run wild. This is one hour when you're allowed to fantasize, dream big, really explore all the infinite possibilities of what your life could be like without being hindered by the usual practical considerations.

Don't worry—if you dream up a fantasy of running off to Spain to become a flamenco dancer, that doesn't mean you will! This is not a process where you make decisions or plans. This exercise has an entirely different purpose. So don't focus on what's reasonably achievable or makes logical sense. Let your mind run free. Think and ponder, or journal, draw, or make lists, or write in a stream of consciousness about all the dreams you'd have for your life if there were no restrictions.

You don't have to come to any conclusions as a result of this dreamtime practice. Just doing it is like medicine for you and will support results down the road. Here's one way to understand this exercise: In the winter, in most climates, it looks like nothing is growing. But we know that's not true. We know that deep down in the cold wet soil, the seeds are soaking in the rich nutrients, building strength, so that when spring comes and it's time to sprout, the deep vitality they've accumulated over time makes them easily able to push through the soil and grow to their fullest potential.

In the same way, for your own goals and desires, the initial stage should not be about plans or practicalities or deciding what to "do." Instead, you first need to "be"—let your dreams gather strength, and fertilize them with your imagination. The fantasies and dreams you're having during this hour are rich nutrients for your future, so that when it *is* time to take action, your dreams will transform into a realistic vision that may not seem at all related to your original fantasy. In every case, however, just like the plants in the spring, you'll have developed powerful energy to help you reach *your* full potential.

THREE DON'TS—WHAT NOT TO DO THIS WEEK

Avoid the following activities because they'd work against your progress.

1. Don't pay attention to a schedule.

As much as possible, avoid a strict schedule. Let go of watching the clock and rushing to one appointment after the other. Whenever you can, let yourself flow through the day according to your own mood. And if for even one day this week, you can turn off the alarm and just wake up when it's natural for you, that'd be helpful too!

2. Don't take care of so many obligations.

Try to find ways to free up more time for yourself and devote less time to the needs of family, friends, or career. It's only for seven days! For instance, delegate as many of your household chores as you can to someone else, reduce any regular calls or visits that friends or relatives expect you to make, and don't work overtime at your job.

3. Don't overexert yourself.

You don't need to stop exercising, but do eliminate any intense or demanding exercise. For instance, strength training, weightlifting, or any exercise that makes you stress and strain is not a good match for the energy of Week One.

TOP 10 DOABLES

These are the activities for Week One that will support your progress and still fit into your already busy schedule. You don't have to do all of them, but any that you do will benefit you in this important stage. Remember, do these for only seven days.

1. **Surround yourself with images of water.** Find a picture of the ocean, a river, lake, etc., and make it the background on your phone or computer, or place that kind of artwork

on your wall or desk. You can also spend time in view of actual water; for instance, take a walk along the shore.

2. **Take a long relaxing soak** in the bathtub or hot tub, go for a swim, or have a session in a float tank. (Taking a shower doesn't qualify because you have to be fully immersed in water.) Whatever activity you choose, remember that relaxing, not stimulating, is the feeling we're aiming for this week.

3. **Do exercise that has a slow flow to it,** such as qi gong, tai chi, yoga, slow dancing, or skating, or just a wandering walk to explore the neighborhood.

4. **Let your creative juices flow.** Paint, sketch, write, dance, play a musical instrument, or even just doodle while you're on the phone. Don't worry about the results. The medicine here is the activity of being creative, not the outcome. And this is just for you—no one else has to see what you create.

5. **Add black.** Add more touches of black to what you wear this week. You don't need to dress in black from head to toe; you can add it in subtle ways, such as in a necklace or handbag. Use more of this color in the décor in your home, such as a black vase on the mantle, or a black towel in the bathroom.

6. **Read fiction** instead of nonfiction. Watch movies instead of the news or documentaries. Listen to podcasts that tell stories instead of any informational ones.

7. **Keep a dream journal.** You may not normally remember your dreams, but try this: The instant you wake up, record even any little shreds of memories you still have. You might record on your phone, or scribble notes on a pad by your bed. What you'll find is that soon, you'll start to remember more and more of your dreams. Don't worry about trying to interpret their meaning—this is not about dream analysis but about opening more to that different source of consciousness.

8. **Stay well-hydrated.** Make sure you're drinking plenty of healthy fluids as you go through your day, but avoid iced drinks in favor of hot, warm, or room-temperature beverages.

9. **Let your inner nonconformist come out!** Say no more often. As much as you can, do things your own way, and not how someone tells you to. Pay more attention to doing what you're in the mood for, rather than what's next on your list.

10. **Get more sleep and spend more time in solitude.** I'm sure you're busy, but make it a priority to get as much sleep as you can this week. During your waking hours, make opportunities for silence and solitude. This is like medicine for you right now, so don't feel selfish for doing it, or think you're wasting time. Doing this actually makes a distinct change in your energy that builds the foundation for our work together in the next stage.

YOUR ONE ESSENTIAL CHOICE FOR WEEK ONE: TRUST

Each of these five weeks has one guiding principle for you to lean on during this stage. If you ground yourself in this one essential choice over the next seven days, you'll make the most progress. This week, look for every opportunity to choose to trust. Here are some examples of what you can do:

Trust your intuition.

If you get a feeling about someone or something, don't discount it just because there's no logical reason you should feel that way. Start out by trusting your gut instinct in that situation and then notice what happens from there. You may well find your intuition was right on. Don't make an important decision on intuition alone, or act impulsively based on a feeling. But listen more often to that small quiet voice inside that's trying to guide you. Notice any subtle feelings you get that you might normally disregard. Pay attention to your instincts to guide you more than you usually would. You might even want to start a journal specifically to record your intuitive impressions, to track them over time and see if they did indeed have messages for you.

Trust the people you should.

Who in your life do you feel is wise beyond their years, or whose experience and knowledge do you feel you should listen to? You're not all alone in your situation. Reach out to the person or people in your life who fall into the category of wise ones. Take the risk to trust a little more than you usually would, explain what's going on for you right now, and ask them to share their advice for you.

This person could be an older friend or family member, a therapist, or a professional consultant who has expertise in what you need help with. If you have an intuitive advisor or a psychic you respect, or if there's one you've heard good things about, this would be a great time to have a session with them. However, no intuitive is 100 percent accurate, so if they tell you something that doesn't resonate with you, pay attention to that, and don't doubt your own sense of things. (Refer back to "trust your intuition!")

Trust Life.

As my wonderful friend Louise Hay used to say, "Life loves you." Life *wants* us to succeed, to have a wonderful, rich, fulfilling experience. It's *we* who tend to get in our own way, sabotage ourselves, or create problems based on old patterns we're still carrying from our past.

If there's something you want to change or achieve, can you put your request out and then let go and trust that Life will help bring you what you need, perhaps in even more wonderful ways than you had hoped for? Watch for signs, small developments or synchronicities that you'd normally overlook or disregard. You can be trying so hard to go in one direction that you're not noticing how Life is trying to guide you toward a different, even better path.

Think of the practice of trust like taking a vitamin to strengthen your system so that the next step in your journey here will take you even farther. What you currently think you want may actually be smaller than what Life can bring you. By doing these exercises over these seven days, you're allowing the power to build and the floodgates to open so Life can deliver to you an even more positive future than it may be possible for you to imagine at this point.

Remember, these assignments are for Week One only. Enjoy your work with them, and watch for any subtle signs or coincidences that you'd might normally overlook or disregard. They might very well be showing you that things are already shifting, possibly in ways you're not expecting!

Chapter 16

WEEK TWO: ACTIVATE YOUR WOOD ELEMENT

If you've not yet completed all seven days of the steps for Week One consecutively, please do not continue on to Week Two until you do. There's an order to the way you need to do this program and you won't get the results you could otherwise if you shortchange yourself, skip back and forth, or don't do the full week's work.

But if you're ready, what you'll find below are your assignments for Week Two. Remember, they're based on using the principles of ancient Chinese medicine, but in a way that addresses the entirety of your life. There are scientific principles underlying these seemingly minor actions that are designed to change how things go for you from here!

THREE STEPS TO TAKE RIGHT NOW

These are the single most important yet easily achievable actions for this week.

1. Spend 30 minutes in nature every day.

In Chinese medicine, being out in nature provides a strong boost for the kind of energy you need at this stage. Ideally, spend this time around trees. It can be a walk through your neighborhood, or a hike in the woods, or just sit under a tree and read a book if the weather allows.

The Japanese call it "forest bathing"—just being in the presence of trees, immersed in their invisible nourishing qi. Research has found this has definite benefits for stress reduction and mental and physical health. (This is not why I'm giving you this assignment, but if you need to convince yourself, you can use it as a reason!)

It doesn't matter whether there are leaves on the trees, and if there aren't many trees where you live, that's not a problem either. Just being out in nature is the most important part of this practice. And if the weather is just too cold or hot or otherwise inclement to be outdoors, spending time in a conservatory, an indoor botanical garden, or a garden store full of green plants is a perfectly acceptable substitute.

2. Make a list of what you want.

This list needs to be of what you *want*, not of what you have to *do*. In other words, don't turn this into a list of chores, or a tally of the steps you have to take to achieve your goals.

Also watch out for feelings of guilt, or worry about being selfish that can prevent you from really feeling free to think about your desires. If you cave in to those unhelpful emotions, this practice won't have the powerful results it's designed for.

Here are some examples of what should NOT go on your list:

- Finish my degree.
- Clean the kitchen.
- Post my online dating profile.
- Stick to my diet.
- Start getting up earlier.

Write this list by hand on paper. Do not type it into a computer or device. It must be in your own handwriting. Begin every line of your list with the words "I want" and be as specific as possible. Nothing is too small to put on your list. Here are some examples of things that might go on the list of what you want:

- I want to live in Italy.
- I want someone to love me.
- I want potato chips.
- I want to earn $10,000 more next year.
- I want to write a book.
- I want to change my hair.
- I want a white kitchen.

Ideally, this list will have *at least* 20 statements and hopefully many, many more. Feel free to fill up several sheets of paper. You can complete it all at once, or you can come back to it throughout the week and add more notes.

Again, don't worry about seeming self-centered or greedy, because in this exercise you're meant to focus on your desires! This is private, just for you. You don't need to show it to anyone or use it for any other purpose—just working on this assignment affects your energy. But if you hold back, the results won't be as powerful, so give yourself permission to go for it.

3. Be "linear."

Here are some ways you can be linear:

- **Activities:** Your activities should be in "straight lines." For example, if you go for a walk, don't go on a wandering walk with no particular destination or time limit. Instead, walk for 20 minutes in one direction and then turn around and walk for 20 minutes back home. When you go grocery shopping, take a list and get only the things on your list. Once that's done, *leave the store.* You're not to continue to wander around and explore the store or buy more things.

- **Keep a new kind of to-do list.** You may already keep a to-do list, but there's a particular way to handle it this week. Create a brand-new list each day, and as you complete a task, *be sure to cross it off the list*. It's best to list only things that can be completed during one day, so, break down any long-term task into smaller steps. In other words, don't write: "Plan our vacation." Break that down into: "Ask Jessica what hotel she stayed at in San Francisco," "Check airfares to SFO in May," "Ask boss for time off May 18–26," "Check airport shuttles at SFO."

- **Stick to a schedule.** Set defined times for as many activities as possible. For instance, schedule your exercise, your meals, when you wake up and when you go to sleep—and stick to that. If you've decided that 5 P.M. is when you'll quit work for the day, then that's that.

THREE DON'TS—WHAT NOT TO DO THIS WEEK

Avoid the following activities because they would work against you this week.

1. Don't stay up past 11 P.M.

Unless you work the night shift, be in bed with eyes closed no later than 11 P.M. for the following seven days. Chinese medicine discovered long ago that our bodies move through certain energy cycles in each 24-hour period. If we align with those cycles, we stay in balance and can more easily solve our problems and achieve our goals.

At 11 P.M. your entire system shifts into the exact frequency that we're boosting during this Week Two. But if you're awake during that time, you don't benefit. If this is much earlier than your normal routine, you may need to ease into it by turning off the TV and any other screens by 10:30 at the latest so your system can begin to relax. You can't expect to abruptly get up from your computer and fall asleep!

2. Don't stay quiet.

It's important this week to speak up! If your friends are trying to decide where to go for lunch and you're craving curry, don't be polite and say, "I'm fine with whatever you'd like!" Say, "I'd *love* some Indian food!" Every day this week, notice even small situations where you'd normally stay quiet and instead speak up—voice your opinion, ask for what you want, or offer an idea in a discussion.

3. Don't take a break from exercise.

If your usual routine is outdoor exercise but the weather is bad, don't use that as an excuse to not work out. Do indoor exercise, clean the house, stay in motion in some way. If you're tired or stressed and just want a break, still push yourself to do some sort of physical movement anyhow. It's only for this week!

And if it's really, *really* not possible to exercise every day this week, then substitute mental exercise instead. Do a crossword puzzle, analyze solutions to a problem, or play a game on your phone or device that takes some thought and strategizing to perform.

TOP 10 DOABLES

These are the activities for Week Two that will support your progress and still fit into your already busy schedule. You don't have to do all of them, but any that you do will support your progress at this important stage. Remember, do these for only seven days.

1. **Place images of trees within frequent sight.** Find a picture of a single tree or an entire forest and make it the background on your phone or computer, or place artwork of it on your wall or desk. You could even plant a seedling in a pot or somewhere outside visible from your window.

2. **Emphasize practicality.** Every day this week, your priority should be using your common sense to make decisions. Ask yourself, "Is this practical, logical, efficient? Does it save me time or money or make my life easier in some way?"

3. **Do exercise that requires some effort.** Workouts that match the energy this week are things like strength training or weight lifting or anything that makes your body exert effort. Or challenge yourself in some way—compete with yourself to try to beat your best time, or participate in competitive sports.

4. **Sing, shout, make noise!** Sing in the shower, or shout your frustrations into a pillow or into the wind outdoors. Bang pots and pans in the kitchen or pound tools as you fix or build something. Play percussion instruments like drums, or even just tap your fingers as you think about a problem.

5. **Add the color green to your life.** It can be any shade of green, from khaki to moss to emerald. If you like how you look in green, then wear more of that color this week. Add green to your home and office in small ways—perhaps a plant for your desk, or artwork with green in it, or a green throw for the couch.

6. **Learn something new.** Read a how-to book, take a class, or teach yourself some new skill. It doesn't have to be anything big or important. You might just try a new recipe or cooking technique, or download a new app and figure out how it works.

7. **Volunteer.** This exercise is about doing something for a cause you believe in. You might volunteer your time to a charity for at least a couple of hours this week, or donate money to a nonprofit, help them raise funds, or actively tell other people about their good work.

8. **Clean up your diet.** For this week, no processed food or fast food! Eat lots of green vegetables and fresh-cooked food or salads. Citrus fruit, fermented vegetables, or vinegary foods like pickles are also good to add, if your diet allows them.

9. **Build something or fix something.** Find a small simple project that you have a very good chance of succeeding at, depending on your skill level. For example, put together an IKEA bookcase, tighten a wobbly doorknob, or mend a piece of clothing.

10. **Create a vision board.** Cut pictures out of magazines, print them from the internet, or draw them yourself, and put them together as a vision board of what you want your future to look like. Or post these images on social media, as long as you'll view them frequently. You can do this all in one sitting or add to it over the next seven days.

YOUR ONE ESSENTIAL CHOICE FOR WEEK TWO: CONFIDENCE

This week, the most important guidance is to look for any opportunity you can to feel a sense of confidence. Here are some examples of what you can do for the next seven days:

Say yes.

This week, choose to have the confidence to say yes to most things. In other words, at times when you'd normally think to yourself, *I'm not sure I can do that*, decide to give it a try. Challenge yourself a little. It might be saying yes to going to a party even if you don't know anyone there, driving to a part of town you're not familiar with, or agreeing to take on a project that you're not sure how to approach.

As you say yes to something, tell yourself, *I can figure it out*. And then do what you need to do to figure it out. For instance, think of a strategy for the party so you can start conversations with people. Look at a map before you drive to that unknown neighborhood even though you have GPS. Strategize ways to approach that project.

Of course you're not going to say yes to anything that's dangerous or way beyond your capabilities. Be realistic, but lean toward a yes this week rather than your usual "Maybe" or "Let me think about it," or "Oh, I couldn't possibly!"

"I was right!"

Compile a list of different times in the past when you thought the best choice would be X and in fact it turned out to be. Think back to when you made a decision and took action, even though you weren't entirely sure what the outcome would be and things actually worked out fine. Remember situations when your sense about someone was correct. Recall the advice you've given to others that you know was right for them, even if they didn't follow it. Think about any times when you took a bit of a risk, maybe did something outside your comfort zone, or where you didn't know all the facts. At the time, you likely said to yourself some version of, "Well, no matter what happens, I can probably manage." And don't limit what you write down to only impressive results! Add situations where in looking back, you see you were right in your view of a person, situation, or problem, even if you failed to act on it at the time.

Notice your successes.

You accomplish so many things each day that you just finish and move on, but that you don't stop to acknowledge or own. Your work this week is to observe as you go through your day, and really notice each accomplishment, each little achievement. And even though you may at first feel silly doing it, every time you finish a task, take a deep breath and say to yourself, "I did it!" before you move on to the next thing. Really let a feeling of success soak in for a few seconds.

At the end of each day this week, take a few minutes to think back to what you got done that day. This is a very different practice than what we usually do, which is to think about everything that still needs to be done or what's coming up tomorrow. Let yourself notice as often as possible how much you actually achieved, and allow that feeling to really sink in. This acts to strengthen your belief in your own decisions and abilities, and builds your muscles for the next stage of work.

This week, continue to watch for signs, small developments, or synchronicities that you'd normally not pay much attention to. These small actions you're taking this week can stimulate a big response from Life. Remember, these assignments are for Week Two only. Enjoy your work with them!

Chapter 17

WEEK THREE: REIGNITE YOUR FIRE ELEMENT

What you'll find below are your assignments for this week. But if you've not yet completed all seven days of the steps for Week Two consecutively, please do not continue on to this week until you do.

As you move forward now, remind yourself that these seemingly illogical assignments *do* have a logic behind them! This is a science that has been proven over thousands of years and is working to influence you, your energy, and your life in a deep and pervasive way.

THREE STEPS TO TAKE RIGHT NOW

These are the single most important yet easily achievable actions for this week.

1. Be spontaneous!

Why? Chinese medicine discovered the cumulative phases of how energy moves through any system, including an individual's personal growth and ability to create change. And at this stage in the process, it's time to align with an energy that's starting to quicken as a result of your previous weeks' work.

Being spontaneous means allowing yourself to take a vacation from how you usually do things. Perhaps normally, you need to think about even a minor decision before choosing whether to do it or not. For instance, a friend texts, asking you to go out to dinner with her on Friday. This might be some version of your usual thought process: *What is my Friday schedule like? Will I be too tired at the end of that day? Am I really in the mood to spend time with her or is there something else I'd rather do that night? Do I have to get a babysitter? Will the commute be especially bad on a Friday night? What do I have to do the next morning that I might need to get up early for and would it limit how much time I could spend with her? What restaurant does she want to go to? Is it too expensive, or is the food not my favorite? If so, what are some options to suggest instead?* (And depending on how analytical a person you are, there might be more!)

So, being spontaneous means breaking free from all the analysis for these seven days. Instead, if your friend asks if you want to do dinner on Friday, what is your immediate emotional reaction? In that *moment*, do you feel a little thrill inside, or is it more like a "meh"? Base your decision on *that* and let everything else go; it'll all get figured out.

If you come home from work and suddenly feel like chucking your usual evening plans and going to a movie, or pulling out your sketchbook and letting your creativity come out to play—do it!

This week, let your heart be your guide. Look for tiny opportunities as you go through your day to be spontaneous, to do what lights you up. Of course your head still needs to be involved; you shouldn't choose to do anything dangerous or careless or hurtful. But this week, even with your smallest choices and decisions, ask yourself, "Which one makes my heart sing?" And as often as possible, do that!

2. Hand out compliments.

Look for every opportunity to compliment people. The compliments need to be genuine and heartfelt, but they can be about very minor things. For instance, at the checkout line at the grocery store, compliment the clerk on how well he does his job. Admire the photo on a co-worker's office wall. Tell a friend you like her new shoes. When you see a parent pushing a stroller, stop to gush over the baby. If you meet someone walking a dog, tell its human what a cute animal it is. Exclaim to a beautiful flower, "You're gorgeous!"

This assignment is not to just hand out a couple of compliments a day! I promise you that your day is *filled* with moments when you could make someone feel special. Every interaction—whether in the elevator, on the phone, or walking down the street—opens a chance to compliment another person. And of course, it's very likely that when you compliment someone, they'll give you one in return. Your job at that point is to say, "Thank you!" and *not* some version of "Oh, this old thing?" Reciprocation is an important part of the process.

3. Cultivate a sense of wonder and delight.

Look for ways to experience the feeling that makes you gasp and say something like "Oh, wow!" It's possible that you immediately think, "Well that sounds nice but I'd need to travel someplace special to have that kind of awe-inspiring experience." Visions of the Grand Canyon or the Pyramids of Giza may come to mind. And sure, if you can manage to visit someplace amazing this week, that'd be great. But what I'm actually talking about is starting to notice how often in your normal daily life you can witness something that makes you feel this way.

If you're in a winter climate right now, it might be the ice crystals on the window that form a tiny work of art. If plants are growing where you live right now, stop and really look at a leaf or flower. Notice the details of its design or the lushness of the colors, and feel a sense of amazement at how even something so minor is a miracle of design.

If you're a parent, observe your child and feel your heart fill with wonder just over the fact of their existence. If you live with an animal, marvel over the beauty of their body or look into their eyes and thrill at feeling a heart connection with another living being. As you do this practice, you'll have increasingly frequent experiences throughout your day that make your spirit sing. Remember that these Week Three assignments nourish a new energy in your system that takes the work you did in the two previous weeks to the next level.

THREE DON'TS—WHAT NOT TO DO THIS WEEK

Avoid the following activities because they would work against you this week.

1. Don't be too practical.

This week is not the time to focus on what's practical, logical, or efficient. It's about listening to your heart more than your analytical left brain. If you feel a little spark of joy inside when you get an idea, then your first response should be "Yes!" and don't let your thoughts start to second-guess that feeling.

2. Don't stuff your feelings.

How often do you feel an emotion rising in your system, but you don't express it? Do you just push it down because you don't want to rock the boat, or because you worry the person you're with won't understand, or worse, will react negatively if you do try to communicate how you're feeling?

Every day this week, notice even small situations where you'd normally stuff a feeling back down inside, and instead, allow yourself to feel it, and if possible, talk about it. Of course, don't say something hurtful because you're in a bad mood, or start an argument because Jean told you to communicate your feelings!

First and foremost, let *yourself* feel your feelings. Don't suppress them; let each feeling come, feel it fully, and then let it move on. That's how our emotions are supposed to journey through our system. "E-motion" = Energy in motion! Then, whenever you can, give yourself a chance to express what you're feeling to someone you feel safe with. It may be a wonderful relief to get it out. And you may be surprised to get a more empathetic response than you thought you might, or one that gives you new insights, or that your relationship with them improves as a result.

3. Don't forget to smile.

Our faces both reflect how we feel and affect how we feel. I'm not asking you to smile because it's a social norm. I'm asking you to smile more frequently because it directly affects your energy. Look for reasons to smile. You don't have to be smiling *at* someone. You can just smile to yourself. And now and then, as you go through your day, check in on how you're holding your mouth. Our mouths are where we tend to hold our tense and unhappy feelings. Each time you relax your lips and give yourself the gift of a smile, it acts to rewire your system in a way that's healing at this stage of the program.

TOP 10 DOABLES

These are the activities for Week Three that will support your progress and still fit into your already busy schedule! You don't have to do all of them, but any that you do will be like vitamins for you at this important stage. Remember, do these for only seven days.

1. **Add any of these colors to your life: red, purple, bright orange, or hot pink.** If you like how you look in any of these colors, then wear them more often for the next seven days. Place touches of them in the décor of your home or office in subtle ways; for example, red apples in a bowl.

2. **Add things that sparkle or flicker.** Hang a crystal in the window so it sparkles in the sunlight and makes rainbows on your walls. Wear sparkly jewelry or a T-shirt with sequins. Burn candles or have a fire in the fireplace.

3. **Speed up!** Exercise that matches the energy this week is something fast-paced and fun. Examples are a Zumba class, salsa dancing, speed walking, or working out to music with a fast beat.

4. **Add variety to your meals.** Change it up when it comes to mealtimes. Try some new cuisine you've never had before. Eat dessert first and salad last. Have an entire meal of hors d'oeuvres. Make sure you eat plenty of brightly colored vegetables. Have fun with your food!

5. **Play.** This is not the time to be weighed down by responsibilities and to-dos but to get in touch with your sense of fun and lightheartedness! This week, look for opportunities to play. You might romp with your kids or play with your cat or take the afternoon off and do something fun. Got to clean the house? Turn up the music and make the work into play!

6. **Go to a live performance.** At least once this week, go to a concert, a theater performance, a lecture, or a free author reading at the local bookstore. Or visit an art gallery or museum to see original art (this carries the live qi of the artist). Experiencing the in-person energy of a performer/creator/artist is the medicine here.

7. **Talk, talk, talk.** Don't hold back—look for ways to express yourself, communicate with others, chat and socialize, even if it's just small talk for 30 seconds as you ride the elevator.

8. **Passion!** Yes, that can include great sex! But really, it has as much to do with feeling any thrill of excitement surge through your system. What are you passionate about? If it's skiing, but you don't have time to schedule in a ski trip this week, well, as least you can plan one. Even if you don't actually go on the trip, the thrill of thinking about it can be like vitamins for you right now.

9. **Find excuses to laugh!** Go to a comedy club, watch funny videos, or read humorous books. Call your friend who makes you laugh so hard you're on the floor. Hang out with people who have a good sense of humor as often as possible, and let yourself have fun.

10. **Get inspired.** What makes your spirit soar? Read inspirational books, watch films, or listen to audios that lift your heart. Take a class about something that's always fascinated you. Get excited about possibilities, even if at this point, they just seem like pie in the sky. What would you *love* to do, even if you know it's totally unrealistic? Start a theater group? Learn to sing? Move to Thailand? Whatever excites you, allow yourself the joy of playing with it in your mind.

YOUR ONE ESSENTIAL CHOICE FOR WEEK THREE: "WHAT DOES MY HEART SAY?"

In Chinese medicine, the energy at this point in your process has to do with the guidance of the heart. But our work-a-day culture constantly directs our attention into our heads, not our hearts, so this may take some conscious effort on your part, to remember to make the shift. As frequently as you can this week, when faced with a choice, a decision, or a problem, notice how you immediately go up into your head to think about it. In that moment, as soon as you notice what's happening, try to catch yourself! And instead, do this:

- Imagine your attention like a light coming down from your head into your heart. (You can still leave some energy up in your head too!)
- Take a deep breath.
- Feel a warmth and a glowing light filling the center of your heart.
- Take a few moments to really let your energy and attention relax into your heart.
- Ask yourself, *What does my heart say?*
- What feeling, image, sensation, or message do you instantly get?
- It may not be a crystal-clear answer, but that's okay. Just get in touch with the feeling, no matter how vague. This is important practice in listening to your heart that will create a shift in your system to positively affect how you deal with the situation and beyond.

This may seem like a very minor practice, especially if you happened to notice that in the instructions above, I didn't say to act on what your heart told you to do! But don't underestimate its power. Just learning to send your awareness to your heart transforms you on more levels than you know, and it takes you much further along on this path of bringing your Five Elements into balance.

As always, this week, watch for signs, small developments, or synchronicities that you'd normally overlook or disregard. These small actions you're taking can stimulate a surprising response from Life! Remember, these assignments are for Week Three only. Enjoy your work with them!

Chapter 18

WEEK FOUR: GROUND YOUR EARTH ELEMENT

Here we are at Week Four, and I hope you've been enjoying this journey! If you've completed all seven days for Week Three, now you can move to this next stage.

Hopefully, you've been able to trust the process more and more as you go along. Keep in mind that what you're doing here is realigning your energy with the energy of nature. This helps the path unfold before you, instead of your having to labor at trying to figure out how to create it all by yourself.

Okay, here we go! Read on to find out what to do—and not do— in Week Four!

THREE STEPS TO TAKE RIGHT NOW

These are the single most important yet easily achievable actions for this week.

1. Practice self-care.

When you read the word *self-care*, you may think, *I already do that. I have a healthy diet, try to exercise regularly and usually get enough sleep.* Or you may think, *Yeah, I really need to eat better and go to bed earlier. And I have to get more disciplined about exercise too.* But actually, these kinds of things aren't what I'm asking you to focus on this week in terms of self-care.

Here, self-care is more about kindness toward yourself. It has to do with taking care of your needs and having better boundaries in terms of taking care of *everyone else's* needs. This is about reducing the time, energy, and attention you give to the *should*s in life and increasing your own personal enjoyment and sense of fulfillment.

It's very possible that there are multiple times in your day when you make small, seemingly inconsequential choices to set your own needs aside to take care of something for someone else, or to get work done at your job or at home. These will be such minor decisions that you probably don't even notice you're making them, but they compound and build on each other to weaken the energy of self-care in your life. In Chinese medicine, this translates directly to weakening your ability to bring your goals and dreams into fruition, so this is far more important than you might have imagined.

This week, whenever you can, catch yourself as you're about to make a choice to set your own needs aside, even if you don't think it's an inconvenience or a big deal. When you become aware that you're about to make that decision, ask yourself, *Is this self-care or* other-*care?*

Then consider other options. For instance, at work, when someone asks you for help at even a slightly inconvenient time, can you say no? Or "I can't help you right now, but how about at three this afternoon?" Or "I'm swamped right now, but I bet William could help you."

At home, consider just how much of your time and energy you actually need to give to taking care of the house and family. Are you letting your daughter's bedtime rituals take more time than is even helpful for her, just out of guilt? Are you making your husband's lunch even though he's not sharing the load of household chores as it is? Are your kids old enough now to help out more around the house but you haven't updated their list of tasks to match their growing capabilities? Maybe it's time for a new plan. Even small changes can be healing for you here.

2. Eat breakfast.

You may never eat breakfast because you're not hungry in the morning, so you don't want to have to force yourself to eat at that time. But just the fact that you're not hungry for breakfast reveals an imbalance in Earth Element in your life and makes it even more important to tend to.

You don't have to eat a lumberjack breakfast, but get something in your stomach. Avoid a cold smoothie or other iced drink, because Chinese medicine has found that pouring a cold liquid into your stomach interferes with the digestive process. So choose either hot, warm, or room-temperature food and beverages.

Lastly, if at all possible, it's best to eat breakfast between the hours of 7 and 9 A.M. This is the time period when if your stomach isn't digesting some food, your brain is not digesting thoughts either. What this means is that without food in your stomach, you won't plan out your day well or accomplish what you need to. Even if you don't normally eat breakfast, you may well find that by the end of this week, you're starting to feel more of an appetite in the morning. That'll be a very good sign!

3. Ask for or accept help.

The energy this week also revolves around revising the ratio of giving versus receiving in your life. Many of us excel at the *giving* part of the equation but are incredibly weak with *receiving*! When things are out of balance here, they have a pervasive influence throughout your life in ways that weaken the foundation for where you can go from here, limitting your possibilities.

Sometimes we don't ask for help because we don't want to impose on people. We rationalize it: "She's already so busy, I can't add to her load." But what we don't realize is that it actually makes other people feel good to help! They feel better about themselves and feel closer to you, touched that you chose to ask them and not someone else.

And it's possible that if you look at the big picture of your relationships, you've done favors, given help to friends and family but haven't allowed them to reciprocate. That makes these other people unconsciously uncomfortable and can negatively affect your relationship with them. So asking for their help restores the healthy flow between you.

And then there's the situation where someone offers help even if you didn't ask for it. In that situation, too many people immediately say some version of "Oh, thanks. That's okay. I've got it." You may automatically think it'd be too much trouble to take the time to explain how to do what they'd help with. That may be true, but perhaps less than you assume. If someone offers to help, before you immediately turn them down, take a moment to think if there might in fact be some way you can accept their help.

THREE DON'TS—WHAT NOT TO DO THIS WEEK

Be cautious of the following activities that would work against you this week.

1. Don't skip meals!

The energy this week builds on feeling full and well-nourished. For the next seven days, don't skip any meals. This means that you can't work through lunch and then grab chocolate and coffee at 3 P.M. Don't even *delay* a meal this week. Pay attention to the signals from your stomach; if your body tells you that you need food, then eat.

2. Don't be so disciplined.

This is not a week to push yourself too hard or to force yourself to stick to a strict discipline. Take it easy on yourself; cut yourself a little slack. If you want to skip your workout, give yourself a break. But don't replace it with a project from work or a responsibility you have to someone else. Only take a break so that you can do something you'd enjoy, for yourself, even if it's just putting your feet up and reading a book.

3. Write down your worries.

Worrying works against the Element we're working on rebalancing this week. For these seven days, see if you can catch yourself whenever you're worrying about that same thing for the umpteenth time. Stop and write down exactly what you're worried about and save that note for a time when you can tend to it. Don't skip this step; getting the worry out of your head and onto paper or a screen changes the energy and creates a container for it so your thoughts don't have to hold it.

TOP 10 DOABLES

These are the activities for Week Four that will support your progress and still fit into your already busy schedule! You don't have to do all of them, but any that you do will help you move through this important stage in the best way. Remember, do these for only seven days.

1. **More togetherness.** The energy this week is about connection and community, not alone time. So look for every opportunity to gather with others, whether it's just to join one friend for tea, or to go to a party or a class, or simply hang out with family. You get bonus points if you share a meal with someone, because Earth is about nourishment!

2. **Add these colors to your life: yellow, beige, brown, or soft pink.** If you like how you look in those colors, wear them more often this week. Or add them to your surroundings in simple ways, such as beige sheets on the bed or drinking from a yellow teacup.

3. **Choose comfort.** Wear comfy clothes; avoid anything that's too tight or shoes that pinch. Especially if clothing is tight around the waist, leave it in your closet this week. Choose the cushiest chair to sit in rather than a hard wooden chair.

4. **Surround yourself with Earth images.** The images that align with the energy of Week Four are landscapes, horizons, mountains, meadows, pastures, farms, or pictures of any sort of food. You can also choose photos of gatherings of family and friends. Make these images the background on your phone or computer, or place artwork like this on your wall or desk.

5. **Use your kitchen.** Spend time in the kitchen every day this week, and be sure to cook on the stove each day even if it's just to reheat leftovers or boil water for tea. (Use the stove for this, not the microwave.) Restock your pantry with appetizing options; clean out the fridge and fill it with fresh food.

6. **Look through your photos.** This week is a good time to go through your digital or printed photos and reminisce. Maybe bring in the rest of the family and make it a nice event, enjoying warm memories of times past.

7. **Plan a party or family gathering.** Plan a family reunion, or a party or other get-together with friends at some later date. And if you can actually have people over this week, even better! It can be a casual thing; the point is just to bring people together.

8. **Garden.** If you're doing this program during a time of year that allows it, work out in the garden this week, even if it's just to pull a few weeds. If you're in a wintery climate right now, pore over seed catalogues, and think about what you'd love to plant when spring comes. Even if your home doesn't have an outside area, you can start an herb garden in your kitchen.

9. **Try this one approach to clutter.** I do *not* want you to tackle a major clutter-clearing this week! Just choose one room, or area of a room, or even just a shelf or drawer—in other words, some place that's small and manageable, so it won't take much time or energy.

   Go through that area and select things that fit into both of these two categories: (1) You no longer use or need it; and (2) You can think of someone you can give it to, or a place you can donate it.

In other words, what books, clothes, or objects, etc., have served their purpose in your life and it would be good to pass them along to help someone else? It can be especially difficult to give away the books that were so helpful to you when you read them. But consider that you have already absorbed and digested the information in that book, and if it helped you, perhaps it can do the same for someone else. But whether you go through your books or not, look for any old belongings that someone else could benefit from.

The final step of this process, however, is important. Whatever you choose to pass on to someone else must make it out of the house and into their hands this week! It must not end up in a bag by the door or in the trunk of your car, waiting for the final stage. So keep this a small project so you can complete the process, whether it's donating things at at charity shop or giving your things to friends or family.

10. **Hugs!** Offer more hugs, receive more hugs, ask for hugs this week! Hug a person, hug an animal, hug a pillow, hug a tree. Just hug!

YOUR ONE ESSENTIAL CHOICE FOR WEEK FOUR: "CONTENTMENT"

In Chinese medicine, the energy at this stage of your process has to do with cultivating a sense of contentment. The feeling of contentment is not something most of us are familiar with. Instead, it's more common to try to feel gratitude or happiness. Those are valuable too, but contentment is a very different thing and is the essence of the energy for this week in the program.

What does contentment feel like? Picture a mother sitting in a rocking chair, holding her beloved sleeping baby in her lap, with a relaxed, warm smile on her face. Imagine how you'd feel at the end of the best, most delicious and satisfying meal you've ever eaten. Tune into that feeling you get when you got much more accomplished than you thought you would. And now you're putting your feet up, with a glass of wine or cup of hot cocoa! That sense of "Ahhh, life is good."

Contentment is a combined feeling of fulfillment, satisfaction, relaxation, and enjoyment. But if you think that you don't often feel this way, you're probably right. Our culture conditions us to never feel complete, to always feel like there's more to do. And many of us are also wired to endlessly criticize ourselves. We never feel like we've done well enough to be content with our work . . . or our relationships . . . or where we live . . . or our lives in general. So this week, consciously choose to create moments of contentment, several times a day. It's more about how frequently you have the feeling rather than how long you hold it.

Here are some ways you can practice contentment:

- Sit in your favorite chair and look around at your possessions. Find the things that make you happy or bring back good memories; for instance, the beautiful vase on the mantle or the souvenir from your trip last year. Really enjoy having these things in your space to feed your soul.

- Take a few moments to just sit and rest after a good meal.

- Feel a sense of satisfaction about something you just purchased, like the new shoes you'd been searching for.

- If you live with an animal, cuddle with them, pet them, hold them close and feel their warmth.

- Think back in your life to a time when you completed an important phase. Perhaps it was graduating from college or moving into your first home. Picture that moment when it was all settled and you could allow yourself a nice deep breath and sink into relaxation after a job well done.

By now you know not to underestimate the power of this practice, even though these assignments seem small and subtle. Even if you're not yet noticing obvious results of the work you've been doing, know that in fact things are changing and you may not be recognizing the changes for what they actually are.

This week truly helps to strengthen the foundation you've been building for a new future. Just keep following your Five-Element map. Remember, these assignments are for Week Four only. Enjoy your work with them!

Chapter 19

WEEK FIVE: EMPOWER YOUR METAL ELEMENT

One more week to go—congratulations on reaching this final phase! You're doing great. If you've completed all of the steps for Weeks One through Four, you can move ahead now to complete your last session of this "acupuncture for your spirit." Each assignment you do is like treating acupuncture points to bring balance back to your life as a whole.

Here we go! Read on to find out what to do—and not do—in Week Five!

THREE STEPS TO TAKE RIGHT NOW

These are the single most important yet easily achievable actions for this week.

1. Spend at least one hour every day by yourself, in privacy.

Getting some space *away* from everyone else, some breathing room and privacy, is an important part of the process this week. Take at least an hour each day to get away by yourself, and if you can get more time, even better.

This hour isn't to be spent sitting quietly on the couch with your family while everyone watches TV. It doesn't mean sharing your den in silence with your spouse while you each catch up on work. It means being *alone*! You might spend it in a room with four walls and a closed door, or go to a big open space like a park, where you can sit or wander by yourself.

This time is also not for paying bills, doing chores, or arguing with your mother on the phone! It's to give you space in your mind as well as in your environment. Read a book, write in your journal, meditate, or do any quiet activity that helps you recover from the stress of your day.

2. Rhythm and predictability.

An erratic schedule goes against the energy at this stage. As much as possible, try to create a "sameness" to the flow of your days. For instance, you might choose to eat meals at the same time, get up in the morning and go to bed at night at the same hours. Whatever you can do to move in a predictable rhythm this week will be very supportive of your progress in this phase.

Of course, circumstances can interfere. Your boss may drop a new project in your lap and you have to stay late, or school may call you to come pick up your sick child so you're delayed in eating lunch. Don't worry—it won't hinder your progress if you have to change your plans.

3. Create sacred space.

We do our best to keep our homes clean and organized, though our busy schedules sometimes interfere. And to one degree or the other, most of us carry on an unending battle with clutter, and often feel we're on the losing side. But many people don't even think about the *invisible* clutter in their space! If you're familiar with my book *Clear Home, Clear Heart* or have attended any of my energy-clearing workshops, you know what I mean. There can be stuck or stagnant energy in your home that can cause you to feel tired or affect your emotions, or block the flow of energy and thus prevent new opportunities from entering your life. This week, it's time to address this. Here are some ideas for making your home more of a sacred space:

- **Designate a room, or an area, or even just a chair in your home as "sacred."** Use this place at least a few minutes every day this week for some activity that is peaceful or inspiring. You might write in your journal, or do a guided imagery exercise, or practice qi gong or yoga.

- **Play loud happy music.** Sound can be a space-clearing tool, to break up old energy and infuse the place with some fresh new vibrations. Choose music that you like, and dance around the house too if you want, because movement can also help to break up stagnation in the qi flow.

- **Burn candles.** Place candles in every room in the house; the more the better. As you light each candle, imbue it with the request for what you'd like the change in energy to bring into your life. Send the same request to all the candles, rather than a different one for each candle, because that can get the energy all confused.

    (I don't advise "smudging" your house; in other words, burning sage to try to affect the energy. That technique has only a minimal effect at best, and can actually invisibly muddy the environment even more.)

- **Do a full space clearing.** Create your own space-clearing techniques or follow the step-by-step instructions in my book *Clear Home, Clear Heart* to space-clear your home. Or have a professional space clearing done in person or remotely by someone who's trained and certified. (See the Recommended Resources section.)

You don't need to do everything that's outlined above for creating sacred space, or even any of them. Feel free to come up with your own ideas too.

THREE DON'TS—WHAT NOT TO DO THIS WEEK

Avoid the following activities because they would work against you this week.

1. Don't spend time in crowds or noisy places.

This week, we're paying attention to how you're affected by the invisible energy around you. Whether you feel you're sensitive to this kind of thing or not, you're still subtly influenced by the energy in your surroundings, and it often happens below the level of your awareness. The more people around you, the more your system is stressed by having to cope with all that "information."

And if you do feel like you're sensitive or an empath, even more reason to abide by this "don't"! Avoid busy stores, noisy parties, or any place you know will have lots of people.

2. Don't rush!

It's important to give yourself plenty of lead time for whatever you do. For instance, make sure you have time in the morning to get used to the day. That can mean lingering quietly with a cup of coffee or puttering around the house for a while before you start in on your day. Or leave early for your commute so you have plenty of breathing time, even if traffic is bad.

3. Don't eat fast food.

One major principle this week centers on quality and purity, so focus on high-quality meals this week, whether that's splurging on something fancy or eating more organic food. And if you already avoid fast food, look at other ways you can improve the quality of what you eat.

TOP 10 DOABLES

These are the activities for Week Five that will support your progress and still fit into your already busy schedule! You don't have to do all of them, but any that you do will be valuable at this important stage. Remember, do these for only seven days.

1. **Place images of the sky within frequent sight.** Find images of a blue sky with fluffy white clouds, or a dramatic scene of clouds at sunset, and make it the background on your phone or computer, or place artwork of it on your wall or desk. Don't use images of the dark night sky, however; only choose daytime or twilight scenes.

2. **Emphasize high-quality clothes.** This is the week to pull your fancy silk shirt out of the closet or put on your best cashmere sweater. Avoid fabrics that are rough or scratchy in favor of natural fabrics like soft cotton, silk, or wool, just as long as they feel good on your skin.

3. **Reduce visual clutter.** Everything that's visible in your home or office "talks" to you more loudly than things that are stored away out of sight. The more visual clutter around you, the more the energetic cacophony your system has to contend with.

   However, do not—I repeat, do *not*—launch into a big clutter-clearing project this week! Instead, see if you can make some small changes by reducing the amount of clutter that's visible to you. It can be as simple as moving stuff into closets, drawers, or boxes, even temporarily, so it's out of sight. If you have to bring it out after the seven days is over, so be it.

4. **Get subtle energy work.** This would be a great time to get any kind of subtle energy work, such as acupuncture, energy clearing, flower essences, essential oils or homeopathy, etc. Doing any kind of breathwork practice, such as pranayama (yogic breathing) would also act like medicine for you now.

5. **Add any of these colors to your life: white, gray, metallic (gold, silver, etc.).** Choose clothing with those colors, or wear metal jewelry. Add any of them to your home in small ways—perhaps a silver bowl on the coffee table, or a gray pillow on the couch.

6. **Use fragrance.** Avoid artificially scented products—we want authentic fragrances here, not chemical smells. Wear perfume, or use naturally scented oils, lotions, and bath products. Buy flowers that fill the room with a beautiful aroma. If you can't wear a scent at work, put it on once you get home.

7. **Give a boost to your self-esteem.** Think back through the past 12 months and make a list of your achievements, no matter how small. For instance, you completed a training, reorganized the garage, made a speech, stood by your friend when she was suffering, taught your child how to ride a bike, etc. At first you may not be able to think of much, but once you get going, you may find you have quite a list!

   Then think back through the decades, even back to childhood. What do you feel proud about, no matter how small? Do you still remember when you got your story published in the school newspaper? Recall how that felt. What about when you graduated from college or got your first raise or promotion? Really tune in to the feeling; let your body soak it in. Feeling proud in this way is not an egotistical exercise. It's allowing yourself to own a true sense of achievement.

8. **Spend time in large, open, or high spaces.** It's important for this phase of your process to have a sense of spaciousness and/or height. Anytime this week that you can be in an environment that feels that way to you will help. Examples of large open spaces like this in buildings are museums, airports, or lobbies of large office buildings. Outdoors, anytime you can be in wide-open spaces qualifies. So instead of taking a walk in the woods, choose a big grassy park, the beach, or anyplace that's more open to the sky. As for being in a high space, you could gaze out at the view from an upper story of a building, fly in an airplane, or sit on a hillside or anyplace that gives you a view far off into the distance.

9. **Notice the beauty around you.** Notice the tiny moments where you briefly see something beautiful, but normally might not pay attention because you're too distracted, rushed, or focused on work. Look for any opportunity to pause and become aware as you go through each of the next seven days. Did a bird just swoop by your window in a graceful curve? Can you appreciate the elegant design of your phone, or your car? Wow, take a moment and really observe.

10. **Practice gratitude.** At some point during each day, take a few minutes to write down what you're grateful for that day. Do it whenever it's easy for you—it can be at the start or end of your day, or during a few quiet moments you can take in the middle of the day. You don't have to write about anything big or important. Are you grateful for that first cup of tea in the morning? The smile a stranger gave you? It all counts.

YOUR ONE ESSENTIAL CHOICE FOR WEEK FIVE: "IT'S GOOD ENOUGH"

Every week has one guiding principle to lead you onward during this stage. If you stay focused on this one essential choice over the following seven days, you'll make the most progress. This week, look for every opportunity to tell yourself *It's good enough*. What do I mean by that? Well, if you pay any attention to your inner chatter, you probably know there's too much self-criticism, self-doubt, or self-judgment going on!

Even in your little everyday experiences, there is often that small voice in the back of your mind telling you that you should have done more, or should have done it better, or else you compare your progress to what others have achieved. In other words, you worry that what you did wasn't "good enough." This can create a constant low-level anxiety that can make you self-conscious in your relationships, preventing true intimacy, for example, as well as negatively affect your career.

In life overall, it can stop you from moving forward with your hopes and dreams because you're convinced there's only one right choice, and you'd better find it *and* do it right, or else what you do won't be "good enough." And most of all this tendency can make your energy contract and tighten in a way that not only stresses your system, it blocks the flow of your life physically, emotionally, and spiritually.

So for the next seven days, try to catch yourself, to give yourself conscious moments when you stop and say, "It's good enough." You'll be the one to discern when you're starting to buy into the "not good enough" illusion. Is it the project you've slaved over, and are checking for the fifth time? Can you tell yourself *It's good enough* and send it in? The date you're going on tonight—have you been agonizing over what to wear, your hair or makeup, rehearsing what to say in conversation, etc., all day? Can you let yourself relax into "It's good enough" and just go have the experience?

As you do this practice, you may well run into times where that self-critical voice in your head protests, *No! It's* not *good enough!* As often as you can, recognize that's your anxious self that you've been giving too much power. For this week, your job is to kindly tell them to go sit in the back seat and let you take the wheel.

And as always, this week, watch for signs, small developments, or synchronicities that you'd normally overlook or disregard. These small actions you're taking in Week Five can create shifts in ways you're not expecting.

COMPLETION

After you finish your work for Week Five, you have one more assignment: let go. This is the final movement for Metal Element as well as for the entire Five-Element Cycle so the energy can keep moving. In other words, let go of what you think the results of this program should be. If you're looking for what you thought needed to happen, it's very likely you'll miss recognizing the results that actually show up. Know that your work has been realigning your system with the natural cycles of life, and of how change and growth occurs. You can feel reassured that you've already set the wheels in motion and now you can trust the process to carry you forward.

It can be a foreign experience to think you can just let things be at this point! But in fact, all the work you've done over the past weeks has created a new template for your progress. It may not be till later on that you look back and suddenly connect the dots, to realize that ever since you did this program, a series of things happened, sometimes in ways you'd never have expected, to bring you to a whole new point in life. So, welcome any events, people, or opportunities that show up in the next days and weeks, because they're ones Life is sending you, to help take you in the direction you need to go from here—toward a destination that is probably even more wonderful than the one you've been aiming for all this time.

In the final section of this book, we'll look at how you can use the power of the Five Elements to easily find your way for the rest of your life and to love the journey as you go.

PART IV

CHINESE MEDICINE FOR THE SPIRIT

*The practitioner is ever mindful and trusting that Nature,
allowed to work and flow unimpeded, leads the patient to
health in body, mind, and spirit, just as the rivers flow
naturally and effortlessly towards the ocean.*

—J.R. Worsley

Chapter 20

SUBTLE TRANSMISSIONS

Gloria was an Earth Element woman in her late 50s who had just been through her third bout with breast cancer. She'd recently gotten an all-clear diagnosis from her doctor and had come to me for a reading to discuss what the next stage of her life should be devoted to. As I looked at her personal patterns, I saw so much Earth that I knew I had to first emphasize what a powerful influence this had on her, because it could too easily limit her ability to see possibilities from here. Only when we'd established that foundation of understanding could we then look forward to helping her express her Earth energy in healthy ways and manage the downsides.

I started out by saying, "There's a major pattern here that often creates situations where the person has endless responsibilities, always having to take care of other people's needs, and never getting time for their own. This can result in exhaustion, as well as frustration, like a mother feels when her children are always tugging on her skirt, wanting something, and—"

But Gloria held up her hand and interrupted me. "Yes, yes, I know all that. I *used* to be that way, twenty years ago, but I've done my personal work and I'm not like that anymore."

She leaned forward and went on with such an intensity in her voice that I could feel it in my bones. "What I'm really here to talk about is my *mother*! She's in an assisted living home, and I have to visit her three times a day. She won't eat unless I'm there, and I'm the only one she trusts to fill her prescriptions and do errands for her, so I'm always running to the drugstore and all over town. All I do is take care of her and I have zero time for myself. I'm exhausted and frustrated and totally fed up!"

Although I'm sure it's immediately obvious to you that Gloria had just described the exact situation she'd impatiently denied, she was totally unaware this was so. I gently pointed out to her that this problem was a match for what I'd just mentioned, and added, "Let me check with you—people with this pattern also often feel very unsupported in life. Even though they're always doing for others, they get very little help themselves. And in the rare times someone does try to give them support, they can end up feeling deeply disappointed, like they still didn't get what they need. Have you ever had any experiences like that?"

Gloria snapped, "Of course. It always happens like that." But I could tell she assumed this was everyone's experience, and nothing unique to her life. It's like the goldfish not being able to see the water it's swimming in! Each of us, to one degree or other, is often too close to see the Elemental program we're running and how it's influencing how we perceive all our experiences.

I went on to talk about how the impact of her Earth would make her feel overly obligated to do so much for her mother (and anyone else in her life), and how difficult it can be for someone with this personality type to have boundaries because they're so driven to help others. In other words, it's very hard for them to set limits for just how much they give, as well as to keep people from taking advantage of them. I reassured her that of course her mother needed to be well cared for and gave her ideas for a new strategy for the situation, including not worrying so much about imposing on her sisters who also lived nearby and had offered to help. I suggested creating a schedule to set up periods of time that were hers and hers alone, instead of just letting her mother's needs take over her days. (You may recognize some subtle Wood Element remedies there, such as strategizing, speaking up to make a new plan, as well as setting a structured schedule!)

I also told her that this Earth pattern meant she was an exceptionally kind and giving person, who would only feel happy and fulfilled if she did have someone or something to take care of. By setting limits on how much she had to tend to her mother, she'd free up time and energy to find something new to take care of that would bring true satisfaction and contentment to her life. I went on to describe all the beneficial qualities that were part of her natural design and gave her ideas for creating a life that would be a better fit for her Earthy nature. Lastly, I gave her a Wood Element prescription as homework that would help her take charge of all that overgiving energy! I explained the science behind the recommendations to help her left brain better accept them.

Gloria sat quietly for a few moments, and then said angrily, "I am so disappointed. Here I come to you for help and all you do is tell me things I already dealt with years ago. I've gotten nothing out of this at all." You might think I'd be sitting there with my mouth open, but I'd actually expected this response. It was due to her Earth, so terribly stuck in feeling disappointed and unsupported, that she projected those negative expectations onto all her experiences. I told her I understood why she felt that way but even so, I hoped she would still try even a few of my suggestions, just to see what might happen. She rolled her eyes and heaved an enormous sigh before heading out the door.

Fast-forward six months. I was at the grocery store and saw a man in the produce section who looked familiar. I realized it was Gloria's husband, who'd come with her to one of my bookstore talks the previous year. I went over to say hi and ask how Gloria was. "She's running a little catering business," he said proudly. "It's funny—a few months ago, she suddenly started exercising every day and turned a lot of her mother's care over to her sisters. Then she came up with this catering idea, and she's really getting a kick out of it. I'll tell her you said hi."

Here's what I know for sure: Gloria did *not* go home and think, *Oh well, I might as well give these remedies a try.* She went home still bitter and resentful. But soon after, she suddenly started going for walks, or joined an exercise class. Maybe she pulled a green sweater out of her closet and bought a bunch of new houseplants. And somehow, probably in a phone call with her sister, she spontaneously said something like, "You guys have just got to help out more," and a new plan got formed. As she did this Wood behavior, her Earth gradually came back into balance. Out of the blue one day, she remembered that she used to love to cook for friends and how they always raved and said she should open a restaurant. She decided a restaurant would be far too much responsibility, but doing some catering now and then would be perfect. And off she went, happily devoted to feeding people, yet with good boundaries—a perfect Earth career!

In other words, she had set into play Wood Element remedies without even being conscious that's what she was doing. Subtle magic had happened during our conversation, as under the surface of her awareness, there was a transmission of healing to her spirit that started the process. I frequently sense this taking effect as I work with a client, and sometimes this happens even *before* the session! I can't count the times that I've given a prescription to someone for a certain Element, only to find out they'd started it a day or so before our consultation. For example, I'd recommend Fire, and they'd excitedly say, "Oh my god, just yesterday, I bought a red jacket and signed up for Zumba classes!" Science has shown that energy isn't limited by time, so it's not surprising that the effects of a session can actually start to take place prior to it happening. (For example, the Global Consciousness Project at Princeton University was an impressive experiment in how the influence of an event can be seen before it occurs. See the Recommended Resources section.)

How can this understanding help *you*? For one thing, this means you may receive a transmission just by reading the recommendations in this book. You may find yourself naturally and unconsciously implementing the perfect remedies in your life without having to concentrate so hard on following the steps I laid out! Or, since the changes can begin to happen in advance of your learning how to create them, you might want to look back over the past several days to reflect on what's been catching your attention recently. Do you recognize any new choices, behaviors, or desires you've had, or purchases you've made? For example, as you read through this book, did you decide you need to add some Water Element to your life, but now you suddenly realize that last week, you bought new black towels for the bathroom and began to crave soup? That shows the process has *already started*, and it can be a nice confirmation for you that you're on your way and you should continue the remedy from here.

There's another aspect of the rebalancing process that can help us here as well. In Chinese medicine, master healers are considered to have the ability to create "resonance" with their patients, to establish sympathetic vibrations with them, like one temple bell's ringing causing another to sound in response. The most skilled physicians are able to harmonize their qi with the qi of their patient, and in that magic moment, as their energies resonate together, is when the healing begins. One way to apply this understanding is if you find you're not sure which of the recommendations in this book to choose in order to bring balance back, pay attention to what resonates for you. What parts of a remedy or prescription ring a little bell deep inside, just as you read about it? The "master healer," in this case, is the age-old truth of the Five Elements, resounding in a way your soul recognizes and responds to.

These universal principles are valuable for more than just solving problems. In the next chapter, we'll look at how to use them to guide us throughout our lives, in what you might call the Five-Element Way!

Chapter 21

THE FIVE-ELEMENT WAY

The Five Elements are the choreography we, and all of nature, are dancing to. In fact, we can even see the Five-Element cycle at work in the broader phases we move through as a culture. For instance, we might place this map over large spans of time in our history, seeing Water in the ancient periods when healing practices were immersed in mostly superstitious beliefs and magical thinking. Then over many centuries of human social evolution, we arrived at the Wood stage of the Age of Reason, and then the Industrial Revolution, where we reached a higher stage of consciousness and maturity, but work became mechanized and people were treated as cogs in the machine. It was an era when life was regimented and highly organized—men marched off to work with their briefcases in a race to climb the corporate ladder, while women's roles were to marry and stay home with the children. There was a place for everything and everything in its place. Our view of life was through a linear cause-and-effect filter, and from that came our current Western medical system's approach to the body as a machine with parts to be tinkered with.

But Wood eventually transforms into Fire, and you might say this is the phase our culture is currently in. We can see it in the emergence in the 1960s with "free love" and "sex, drugs, and rock and roll," where the rigid structure started to fall apart. For example, women and minorities began to gain more freedom and expand the possibilities for what they could do in the world. The personal-growth movement took off, with people feeling freer to express their emotions and follow their hearts. But we can also recognize Fire in how society came to value fame so greatly that we began to define success by how much attention someone received, whether or not they had done anything productive at all.

Fire is reflected in how incredibly fast-paced our lives have become, and in all the electronic devices that constantly distract us. (Electricity is Fire.) And the effect of all this technology is the decreasing ability of many of us to focus for more than a handful of seconds, our brains flickering like flames. Research shows our attention spans have been alarmingly shortened, and we can even notice this when we watch scenes in movies and television shows from years past, many of which now seem agonizingly slow to our eyes. We skim along with superficialities, like with online dating, swiping left just because we don't like the look of someone instead of taking the time to get to know them. The vast majority of people don't get enough sleep, whether due to tight schedules or a struggle with insomnia, and their nerves are shot. Heart disease and stroke are the most common causes of death, both Fire Element illnesses. These are just a few of the many, many examples of Fire that we could find affecting our current lives. We've all become overstimulated, a sign that our systems are experiencing some degree of Fire "shock," unable to calm down and become peaceful. Fire energy seems to have built to a peak, and perhaps gotten stuck winding in on itself ever more intensely instead of moving on to the next stage in the cycle.

WAYS TO BRING BALANCE BACK

Even though most people aren't consciously aware of the Five Elements, because this cycle is part of everyone's nature, some unknowingly have been trying to heal the situation by using the Elemental remedy of Water, which controls Fire. For instance, seeing the lack of soul in our present ways of treating illness, some have turned back to ancient practices, trying to use those techniques to heal. But I would offer that this isn't a helpful way to bring in Water as a remedy. We've evolved as people since those times hundreds, even thousands of years ago, and methods that worked at those earlier levels of awareness won't be so effective for our more complex minds and modern experiences, or our current place in human spiritual evolution. Instead, we might look at how to use the deeper wisdom underlying those age-old practices in a more fitting way, rather than use the exact same methods—and, in fact, that's part of what I'm attempting to do with this book.

Yet another way to look at how to heal this imbalance is to remember that the energy in the Five-Element Cycle is meant to continue to progress forward! When we look at the situation in that light, another idea comes to mind—we've emerged from Water, moved through Wood, and then into Fire—now, what about heading toward Earth Element? That's the next stage in the circle, because Fire is meant to transform into Earth. Calling in the settling influence of Earth would certainly help Fire's flame to stop flaring so out of control, and to relax into a calm glow.

What would that be like? Earth Element would help us realize a greater sense of community, with more recognition that we are all connected and all one people on this planet. One benefit Fire has brought us is that technology has allowed us to communicate with and befriend people in all cultures all over the world. A boost to Earth energy would take this to the next step, to embrace everyone as part of our family, to be cared for no matter what they look like, where they live, or what their political or religious beliefs are.

This Element also directs our attention to the ground beneath our feet, and the welfare of Mother Earth. The environmental crises that have been peaking in the Fire phase may now be alarming us enough that we will move to take better care of literal Earth, our home. And speaking of home, this is another aspect of this Element, so we could turn our focus to homelessness, which has also reached emergency levels in the U.S. and many other countries. Finding ways to provide shelter, a warm meal, and a soft bed are all Earth responsibilities.

Earth could also be seen as woman energy (because it's associated with mother). In most cultures, women have gradually claimed more authority over the past decades, and if this could increase, the global balance of power would shift to Earth Element, moving from a masculine approach focused on domination to a feminine one that wants to nurture. We could help this along by choosing leaders who have an Earth nature, whether they're men or women.

To support this global shift toward Earth, we don't have to all start dressing in Earth colors! It's that now we can consciously choose to say yes to anything we recognize as Earth behavior over any other Element's, because that will ease us in the direction we as a people need to go at this stage. So instead of valuing fame, we could value kindness: take all that energy people have been using to seek attention, and instead devote it to doing acts of compassion each day. Any small choice you make to honor Earth energy will work to heal and bring balance back to our global community as a whole, just as an acupuncture needle harmonizes the health of the entire body.

NAVIGATING YOUR OWN LIFE USING THE FIVE-ELEMENT MAP

When these five energies move in their naturally balanced rhythm within your spirit, your life unfolds with ease. You can draw on your courage in difficult times, find your direction in life, experience the joy in the journey, be deeply content with where you end up, and feel honored knowing you're fulfilling your sacred purpose.

And this is the map you can consult any step of the way to make sure you're in the flow, whether it's how you plan your day, work on a project, manage a relationship, or solve a problem. For example, if there's a goal you want to achieve, start with Water—what is the dream beneath the desire for that goal? Is there something deeper there that might inform your choices from here? Take time to develop the idea further, because it's not as ready to be born as you think. Let your thoughts process for a while instead of taking action. And hand it over to your unconscious by sleeping on it or forgetting about it for a few days; focus on something else entirely to give your intuitive brain a chance to do some work that could bring the important insights you need in order to be successful. In fact, the first step with Water should always be: do nothing.

Then move to Wood. Define your goal. Think about it: What is the actual vision? What really is the outcome that you want? Then take some time to plot out the path to get there. Create a logical action plan, chopping it into short, achievable steps to be done on a practical schedule. Don't be impulsive and get going before the plan is fully thought out, but don't procrastinate either. There will be a point in the process where you know enough to make an educated decision. When you reach that point—act! Get going, do something, even if you're not completely confident you know what you're doing.

Then let Fire flare. Stay in touch with your original excitement about your idea; don't be too focused on going headlong toward the goal. What makes your heart sing in this process, and how can you have fun while doing it? Maintaining your sense of joy will also help prevent your nerves from being jangled as things naturally speed up and require you to handle several tasks at once. And bring other people to the party, even if it's just talking to them about your experience and what you're trying to achieve, to help keep your passion for this ignited!

Next, settle into Earth. What still needs to be completed? Look around at the little things you should tend to in order to make sure you can bring your dream to fruition. And consider how well your needs are being met at this stage of the work. Are you getting enough help? Have you been trying to go it alone when that might not be the right choice? Stay connected to the community of people who feel like family to you, and be sure you're reaching out for the right kind of support so you can be satisfied with the results of all your hard work.

Finally, go to Metal. Pull back for a big picture view of where you are right now with this project. Does it still feel meaningful to you, or do you need to refine it to make it more aligned with your original dream? Let your body be an instinctual guide at this stage. Notice any physical sensations as you think about each of your possible choices. Do you feel a brightness in your body when you consider one direction and more like an inner thud with another? As you bring the project to a close, allow yourself to feel genuinely proud of your achievement, and then—let go. If you can do that, you may even find you end up with far more rewards than you had first imagined.

This process can be repeated consistently throughout your work on anything, even checking in once a day, to find out what's happening with each Element, and if there are any course corrections you need to make to stay on track. For instance, you might simply ask yourself some version of *Can I surrender and trust that things are happening behind the scenes to move me forward? Do I need to adjust the plan because circumstances have changed? How can I have more fun with this? Am I pausing to give myself moments of satisfaction with what I've completed? Is this still meaningful for me?*

FIVE ELEMENTS EVERYWHERE . . .

Once you've started to learn about the Five Elements, you'll begin to see them everywhere—in aspects of daily life such as the style and colors of the clothes people wear, how they decorate their homes, and how they structure their days, for instance. You'll also discover them in how a business is organized or the themes running through social or political movements. You can even use this knowledge to recognize whether any advice you're being given is thorough enough. Anytime you read an article titled "The Four Steps to Success/Love/Happiness, etc." you will know they missed one!

But what can be most fascinating of all is how you'll find these five energies expressed in the personalities around you. I'm always amazed at how I can see, with breathtaking detail, the way people's Elements weave together to form their patterns of belief, perception, and behavior, their unique strengths and challenges, and what they really need in order to find happiness in life. This gives me the ability to view them with understanding and acceptance, and allows me to help them make choices that align with their true nature.

If you'd like to learn more about how to do this too, I'd recommend reading any of my other books, as well as viewing my online courses. All are available at www.JeanHaner.com. And if you'd like to learn to be a professional Five-Element Coach, reach out to me via the Contact page on my website. You can also find more information about this ancient knowledge in the Recommended Resources at the back of this book. Lastly, I've formed a Five-Element Solution Facebook group to offer you support and guidance so you can always live true to your nature, know how to stay in balance, and to help others do the same! Please join me at www.facebook .com/groups/TheFiveElementSolution.

FOLLOW THE FLOW

Each day, and throughout the course of our lives, we can follow the way of these universal principles as simply as this:

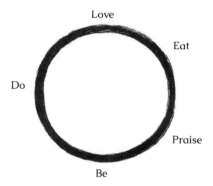

Be–Do–Love–Eat–Praise

Be: Surrender and trust the process, knowing it's not all up to you to make things happen.

Do: Take correct action when the vision is clear and the time is right.

Love: Thrill in the joy of expressing love to others and in feeling endlessly lovable within yourself.

Eat: Chew your life with gusto and get your fill.

Praise: Sing your gratitude to the heavens for each precious, beautiful moment of your life.

APPENDIX

The Five-Element Guides Meditation

There's one last Five-Element gift I'd like to give you: a guided meditation you can use anytime to help with problems and decisions, or just to stay in the flow.

As we have learned, the Five Elements show us the map of everything—including the territory you'll cover as you travel all the days of your life. It can be difficult to know how to navigate this odyssey you're on, but you don't have to do this alone. This book has shown you how your knowledge of these same patterns can assist you all the way along, to make decisions, solve problems, and to maintain balance as you go.

Another way the Elements can be helpful is as five archetypal energies that are both part of the collective consciousness and your unique consciousness too. Together they form a complete support system for you, to guide you toward wisdom, strength, joy, love, and sacred power.

In the following meditation, you will meet these archetypes and receive guidance from them. There are many different ways you can use this practice—you can benefit from it just by following along without any preparation. Or if you're working with a certain issue, trying to make a decision, or have a specific question, then you can approach this experience with that in mind. You can't do this wrong, and you can use this meditation in a different way each time you do it.

So now let's go on a journey to meet your Five-Element guides.

First make sure you're comfortable and in a quiet place. It's best not to do this meditation when you need to be attentive and aware. Save it for a time when there are no distractions.

So, sit in a comfy chair or lie down, and feel yourself start to settle in. Take a nice deep breath. And just relax.

Direct your loving awareness to your face, and feel as if you're soaking in some gentle sunlight that's shining on your skin. Let that warmth soak in, and help all the muscles in your face relax. Be aware of how nice that feels.

Take another deep breath. Then bring your attention down through your neck and shoulders. Let that warm glowing energy flow down from your face now, and feel all the tension in your neck and shoulders begin to melt and let go. Then let it stream down into your arms and then your fingers, all loose and warm.

Feel the weight of gravity on your shoulders and upper body so you start to feel even more heavy and relaxed. Then allow this warm glow to move slowly down through your chest and into the middle of your body for a deep release and relaxation there, like you're sinking into a bathtub full of warm water.

And now all the tension is draining away down through your hips and the base of your body, and that warm feeling is flowing down into your legs, through your knees, to your ankles, and on into your feet and toes. Feel your feet become warm and how delicious that sensation is. Become aware of how much more relaxed your whole body now feels. Take another deep breath.

And now imagine that you're walking around your house and you discover a secret door you never knew was there before this moment. You have just found it—it's been hidden all this time. Stand there and look at the door and notice the grain of the wood and what color it is. Notice the doorknob—what it's made of, what shape it is—and then put your hand on the doorknob and feel the coolness of it in the palm of your hand.

The door is unlocked. Turn the knob and open the door to discover a little stairway up to a room you've never seen before. Step in and close the door behind you. Then go up the stairs and find yourself standing in a cozy room with sunlight streaming in. There are pretty pictures on the wall, a soft colorful rug on the floor, and a big comfy chair set by a window with a view out across the trees and hills.

Walk over to sit down in the chair and snuggle in till you're completely comfortable. The window is slightly open to allow in the sounds of birds chirping outside, and you feel a gentle warm breeze of fresh air across your cheek.

Sit and gaze out the window at the beautiful nature scene outside. Breathe in that sweet-smelling air and realize you haven't had a chance to feel this relaxed in a very long time. Take another deep breath and close your eyes, and when you open them again, you find yourself in a different place.

You're standing on a sandy beach at night. It's a warm night and you can hear the roar of the waves in the dark. Start to walk along the beach, hearing the sound of the waves to your right, and on your left, you can see dimly in the blackness, some high rocky bluffs rising out of the sand. It feels like you're in a dream. Even though it's pitch-black, you easily know where to step and you have no fear of moving forward in the dark.

After a while, off in the distance you start to see a tiny light—it's a torch by an opening in the bluffs. Keep walking till you reach the flaming torch and notice the opening is an entrance to a cave. Deep inside of this cave is the first of your archetypes: the Oracle.

She's waiting for you, so step into the cave, and as you do, you feel the darkness deepen as you leave the light of the torch behind. The roar of the ocean waves becomes a distant rumble as you walk, but now you can hear trickling water, and as your eyes get used to the dark, you can see the glistening rivulets running down the stony walls of the cave. Your eyes can just make out the path as you go and now you see there's a bend ahead, and beyond it, an even darker opening. Continue around the bend and onward into a cavern deep within the cave.

In the cavern, you see a still pool of water glistening in the faint light of two small torches set on either side of massive chair made of rocks rounded smooth by the waves. Seated there is the Oracle. She's a woman with long, flowing dark hair, dressed all in black, with substantial, wide hips, and her feet firmly planted on the stone floor.

She's ancient but she doesn't look so old—she looks plump and vital. She has tremendous reserves to have survived to a very great age. The Oracle has a natural connection to the mysteries; she holds the wisdom of the ages deep in her bones. She has the power to transform fear to courage, doubt to trust. She can transmit to you the strength and wisdom of all the ancestors, all those who have come before you, to help you survive even the most difficult of times. The Oracle sits totally calm, still, and silent, looking into your eyes as you approach her. She's waiting for you to speak. You can consult her for answers to any question.

So take your time now to collect your thoughts and to think about what you might want her guidance for.

Now ask your question, and then wait for her reply. She may speak her answer or she may transmit it directly into your mind. It may be as if you can hear her voice deep inside you, or you may just suddenly feel an inner knowing, or perhaps something will just feel complete. Allow this to process—it may take a few moments to receive her response.

And when that's done, look deep into her eyes and silently thank her. Know you can return here anytime, whenever you need her.

Now turn to go back out—out of the cavern and around the bend into the main cave, and follow that until you step out to emerge from the darkness and discover yourself back on the beach, but it's now morning. A beautiful fresh light is streaming over the landscape and you hear the birds calling overhead.

Walk along until you come to a path that leads gently up off the beach and into a grove of tall trees, their green leaves shimmering in the morning breeze. You can even hear the branches creaking as they sway, and as you go deeper into the woods you see the texture and design of the bark on their trunks. Breathe in the scent of the wood as you walk and feel the crunch of the twigs under your feet.

As you continue, you see ahead on the path that there's the largest of all the trees, soaring far up to create a high canopy of leaves arching above you. And under that tree, someone is waiting for you. It's a tall man with a wiry body, strong eyebrows, piercing eyes, and a sculpted jaw.

This is the Pathfinder. He's like a scout who knows the territory. He's aware of where and how you've traveled in the past, and where you'll need to go as you journey on into your future. He knows the plan for who you're meant to become, and all the winding routes you need to travel to get there. He will guide you in the right direction to make sure you get to your destination.

Go stand next to him and watch as he unfolds an ancient map and holds it up against the trunk of this massive tree. And there it is—this map shows the trails of all the places you've been in the past, all the roads you've covered so far, all the twists and turns that have brought you to this very point. You may feel so reassured that you've been doing it right this whole time, despite your doubts.

He puts his finger on a big red X that says You are here. And then he shows you the path from here. With his finger he traces over the way to go onward for you and it all starts to make sense. Take some time to focus on and discuss with him what he's pointing out. You may be surprised by where you're going, what the plan is from here, and all the curves and bends in the roads, nothing a straight line. Everything starts to come clear now.

If you have a question for this guide, you can ask it. You can point to anyplace on the map in the past, or where you are now, or a spot in the future, to ask any question and get his reply. So think about what you'd like to ask him, and then say it out loud to him. As before, it may take a few seconds to get his reply, and it may be spoken to you, or come in some other form. All you have to do is just relax and stay present.

And when you feel complete, look straight into his eyes and thank him. Know you can always return to this tree to ask for directions. He smiles and then motions you to go farther on through the forest. So walk on and notice the trees begin to thin out until you come to a clearing with the grove finally behind you.

Follow the path onward as it eventually leads you along the side of a tall stone wall. Continue until you see an ancient wooden doorway in the wall. Standing there is the Guardian of the Gate—a radiant woman with big sparkling eyes, curly hair and a welcoming smile on her face.

She takes out an old iron key, inserts it into the lock in the door and motions for you to enter with her. The door swings open to reveal a breathtakingly beautiful garden, filled with vibrant flowers in full bloom, butterflies swooping about and brightly colored birds singing overhead. The sunlight on the leaves makes them glow a brilliant green, the sweet scent of the flowers fills the air, and the gentle warmth of the sun on your face feels like a caress. No matter where you look, you see things that make you gasp with delight.

This is your private garden, and it's protected by the Guardian of the Gate. She knows who you really are in your heart of hearts and you can trust her completely to open the door only to those who will truly love you and honor this magical sacred garden.

Walk around now with the Guardian to explore this place. It all seems strangely familiar to you, and you feel thrilled as little animals come up to you to be petted and played with. You're almost in disbelief that any place could be so full of joy and beauty, and you've never felt so immediately lighthearted.

Sit down with the Guardian under a tree full of blossoms and birdsong. If you have a question about love, or how to keep your heart open despite your current circumstances or past heartbreak, or about how you can feel truly and completely lovable within yourself, this is the time to ask.

So take a few moments to collect your thoughts and then ask her—and receive her answer. Let that guidance rest in your heart.

Then the Guardian takes you by the hand and leads you back toward the doorway again, but along the way she stops and picks the most beautiful and fragrant pink rose, handing it to you as she opens the door and gives you a kiss on the cheek. And as you emerge from the garden carrying your rose, you hear her loving laugh as you each wave goodbye.

As you walk along, still immersed in that glow, you notice a little cottage in the distance. A broad winding path leads to the front door, and as you approach it, the door opens and there stands the Goddess of Compassion, the archetype of the loving mother. She is round and plump with pink cheeks and a big smile on her face, and as you approach, she opens her arms to give you a big hug. She ushers you into the house, and even though you think you've not been there before, it feels like home to you.

The Goddess sits down in a big rocking chair by the fireplace and motions for you to climb up on her lap. Even though you're all grown up, you find yourself really wanting to do that. So go ahead now and climb into her lap. You find there's plenty of room for you, and it's very, very comfortable.

The Goddess of Compassion is the one who will always make it better. She loves and accepts you completely for who you are right now. So let her hold you and hug you and rock you and tell you everything is going to be all right. Relax into her arms, hear her heart beating, and listen to her hum a gentle song as she hugs you. Feel how soft but solid she is and how deeply and completely safe you feel.

A loving mother is the one person in all the world whom you can tell anything that's troubling you. You can be completely open with her. So take some time now to choose something you need to talk about—possibly something you can't share with anyone else.

So do that now—talk to her about something that's troubling you. Let the tears flow if they need to. And what you'll find is that as you speak each word, she soaks it in. With each word, some of the anguish disappears from your spirit and you feel more and more relaxed and safe. Breathe in her sweet warm scent and know that all is well. Let feeling that sink in; stay there for a while, and rest, rest, rest in her arms.

Take a deep breath now, and know that anytime you're in distress, you can come to her. She'll scoop you up and hold you tight and make everything all right. When you feel complete, give her a big hug and thank her, and hand her the pink rose you received at the garden as you bid her farewell for now. She smiles broadly as she walks you back to the door and hugs you one more time.

As you leave, you notice the afternoon has ended and the evening has begun. It's starting to become twilight now, with everything bathed in a pale glow that makes things seem otherworldly. The air is pristine, and you take a deep breath to fill your lungs. A slight breeze feels cool on your skin as you walk onward until you come to a high place where you can see far off into the distant sky.

You feel like you can see forever—the sky is an ethereal blue with soft clouds that makes the scene look like a painting. As you stand there, you become aware of a presence and turn to see an old man approaching. He has a prominent nose and clear eyes, and he projects a sense of power and authority.

This is the archetype of the Sacred Father, who's here to show you the far view, how to achieve your most ideal life, and how to maintain your connection to the divine. Just his presence helps lift your awareness from being too immersed in your mundane daily thoughts. You take a deep breath and feel inspired to raise your sights to your sacred purpose in life.

He motions for you to come stand beside him at the highest viewpoint, and as he extends his arm outward, you feel an immediate sense of spaciousness fill you. In a few moments, you're going to ask him a question of any sort and receive an answer. Don't overthink it—you may just want to ask him the first thing that comes to mind, or there may be a pressing question you feel it's imperative to ask right now.

Either way, take a moment now to formulate your question in your mind. Now turn to look into his benevolent face and ask him what you need to.

His answer to you may be transmitted directly, or as a sensation inside of you, or an image in your mind, but whatever it is, trust that and breathe it in.

Then he turns to point off into the distance, and you see the clouds start to shift in the sky. Slowly, they form images of your far-off and best future, what your life can be like 10, 15, even 20 or more years from now.

Just let the clouds gradually shift and change, and watch for what you can make out. Do you see your future best self? Notice what you're wearing in that distant time, where you're standing, who else is there, and what you're about to go do. Even if it feels like you may just be imagining it, open yourself to the possibility that this may in fact come true.

Suddenly, a beautiful ray of light streams down from the clouds and bathes you in luminescence. You feel all your old regrets evaporating, cleansed in that heavenly light. A growing sense of clarity and purpose flow through your body, even if you don't have the words for it yet.

When you feel complete, turn to look deep into the brilliantly clear eyes of the Sacred Father. He puts his hands on your shoulders and you silently feel how proud of you he is, and that he's conveying his blessing to you.

You both take a long, deep breath at the same time, and then you bow your head to him, and turn to leave, knowing you can always return to this vantage point and summon his presence again in the future.

Walk back down the gentle hillside. It's magic time now, true twilight when the dim light has a purple glow and the world is becoming quiet. It's only a little further on until you find yourself back in the easy chair in that secret hidden room in your own home. Settle in now, close your eyes, and relax. Feel the weight of your bottom in the chair, and gravity heavy on your shoulders as you sit there. Take a deep breath and come back fully into your body.

And now find yourself back where you started, sitting or lying down. Direct your awareness to your face, raise and lower your eyebrows, then form your lips into a smile. Yawn if you feel the urge.

Now let your energy move down from your face to fill your neck and shoulders, through your chest, and down your arms into your hands and fingers. Let it flow down through your torso, warming your stomach, down through your hips and the base of your body, and then feel it flood down into your legs, your knees, then your ankles till it reaches your feet and lights them up all the way to your toes. Wiggle your fingers, wiggle your toes; you are completely back and grounded in your own body right now. You've never felt better; you're in perfect balance. All is well, and you're home.

RECOMMENDED RESOURCES

The Five-Element Solution Facebook Group: This is a group I've created to support you in using the Five Elements to transform your life. Join me there! www.facebook.com/groups/TheFiveElementSolution.

Five-Element Personalities: You can learn more about the Five-Element personality types in my books and courses available at www.JeanHaner.com.

Five-Element Acupuncture: Most of the acupuncture practiced in the world today is referred to as Traditional Chinese Medicine (TCM). But there is actually nothing "traditional" about it, as it only emerged in the 1950s after Mao Zedong—as part of his sweeping purges—stripped the ancient wisdom from Chinese medicine. Practitioners of the classical healing traditions were banned, imprisoned, and even killed. Acupuncture treatments were reduced to very basic applications that rural people could learn to perform as what were called "barefoot doctors." Out of this came most of what is taught worldwide as TCM, and it can indeed successfully treat many health issues. However, it doesn't address the emotional, spiritual, and transformational aspects of illness, which is where all true healing needs to happen.

Fortunately, some of the original knowledge did escape Mao's reach and survives today in some lesser-known forms of acupuncture outside of China. The one I respect and recommend is Five-Element Acupuncture because it addresses transformational healing on the level of the spirit as well as the body. Even if you don't have a health issue, but you want to support your wellness emotionally or spiritually, you might consider working with an acupuncturist who specifically practices Five-Element Acupuncture and not TCM. Five-Element acupuncturists have learned everything TCM practitioners know, and then have gone on for this significantly advanced training.

Space Clearing: Step-by-step instructions on how to space-clear your home can be found in my book *Clear Home, Clear Heart,* or through my workshops. I also do remote space clearings for clients. More info at www.JeanHaner.com/Sessions.

Ancestral Clearing: This is a form of energy work that clears the energy back through both sides of your family line so it's no longer affecting you or future generations. It is always included in Clear Home, Clear Heart retreats, and I do private ancestral clearing sessions for clients as well. More info at www.JeanHaner.com.

Family Constellations: This is a method that addresses the "emotional inheritance" of a dysfunction passed down through the generations of a family. It was originated by German psychotherapist Bert Hellinger, and there are many practitioners of this system available throughout the world.

Louise Hay's book *Mirror Work: 21 Days to Heal Your Life* can be purchased from Hay House, Inc. www.HayHouse.com

Global Consciousness Project: http://noosphere.princeton.edu

RECOMMENDED READING

Archetypal Acupuncture: Healing with the Five Elements by Gary Dolowich

Between Heaven and Earth: A Guide to Chinese Medicine by Harriet Beinfield and Efrem Korngold

Chinese Medicine for Maximum Immunity: Understanding the Five Elemental Types for Health and Well-Being by Jason Elias and Katherine Ketcham

Clear Home Clear Heart: Learn to Clear the Energy of People and Places by Jean Haner

Entangled Minds: Extrasensory Experiences in a Quantum Reality by Dean Radin

Five Spirits: Alchemical Acupuncture for Psychological and Spiritual Healing by Lorie Eve Dechar

Miracles of Mind: Exploring Nonlocal Consciousness and Spiritual Healing by Russell Targ and Jane Katra

Power of the Five Elements: The Chinese Medicine Path to Health Aging and Stress Resistance by Charles A. Moss

Real Love: The Art of Mindful Connection by Sharon Salzberg

Shen: Psycho-Emotional Aspects of Chinese Medicine by Elisa Rossi

Tao: The Watercourse Way by Alan Watts

The Alchemy of Inner Work: A Guide for Turning Illness and Suffering into True Health and Well-Being by Lorie Eve Dechar

The Web That Has No Weaver: Understanding Chinese Medicine by Ted J. Kaptchuk

The Wisdom of Your Face: Change Your Life with Chinese Face Reading! by Jean Haner

The Wisdom of Your Child's Face: Discover Your Child's True Nature with Chinese Face Reading by Jean Haner

The Wise Heart: A Guide to the Universal Teachings of Buddhist Psychology by Jack Kornfield

Wood Becomes Water: Chinese Medicine in Everyday Life by Gail Reichstein

Your Hidden Symmetry: How Your Birth Date Reveals the Plan for Your Life by Jean Haner

ACKNOWLEDGMENTS

As I sit down to think about whom to acknowledge, I know the list could end up being longer than the actual book. It's impossible to thank everyone I owe a deep bow of appreciation to, especially all the teachers and guides who had so much patience with me over the years. When I look back, I wonder why some of them ever put up with me as I achingly, slowly began to explore the world outside the walls of my left-brained analytical comfort zone, and gradually began to surrender, to trust and feel, and become more whole. I still have a long way to go, but when I turn around and look back, I can see how far I've come, and that feels good.

Special thanks to all the Taoist teachers I've studied with, most of whom didn't have the faintest idea they were teaching Taoist principles. A huge thank-you to my exceptionally perceptive editor, Nicolette Salamanca Young, who's always lovely to work with. Loving appreciation to my son Jeffrey Wai-Ming Dong for creating the illustrations for this book. I also owe an enormous debt of gratitude to the friends and family who have provided endless love and support, including most of all Laurel Kelly and John Sims, Diane and Eric Anderson, Roselle Kovitz, Zita Lekeberg, Melanie Mattison, and Ruth Mikos. I lift my eyes to send love and thanks to my parents, Phyllis and Wendall, and to my soul sister Louise Hay, all of whom I miss so much. Lastly, my heart is so full of gratitude for the thousands of teachers I've had over the years who showed up in the form of students and clients. I am the luckiest woman in the world to have been so honored to learn from your stories, and hope I've been able to use that knowledge well enough to help more people with my books and workshops.

ABOUT THE AUTHOR

Jean Haner is the author of *The Wisdom of Your Face, The Wisdom of Your Child's Face, Your Hidden Symmetry,* and *Clear Home, Clear Heart.* She has studied the spiritual principles of Chinese medicine for over 30 years and is known for translating this ancient wisdom into practical solutions for modern problems.

Jean married into a Chinese family when she was in her 20s and first began to learn about Chinese culture, philosophy, and medicine from her very traditional mother-in-law. It wasn't until after her wedding that she discovered the family had her facial features and birth date evaluated to see if she would bring "luck" to them. Jean went on to study the deeper foundations of this ancient knowledge with many teachers over the years, and found it has nothing to do with "luck," and everything to do with learning how to be true to your nature.

Jean teaches workshops and consults individually with people in how to use the Five-Element map to navigate their lives. To learn more and to get information on courses, professional trainings, private sessions, or just to say hi, please visit: www.JeanHaner.com.

Hay House Titles of Related Interest

We hope you enjoyed this Hay House book. If you'd like to receive our online catalog featuring additional information on Hay House books and products, or if you'd like to find out more about the Hay Foundation, please contact:

Hay House, Inc., P.O. Box 5100, Carlsbad, CA 92018-5100
(760) 431-7695 or (800) 654-5126
(760) 431-6948 (fax) or (800) 650-5115 (fax)
www.hayhouse.com® • www.hayfoundation.org

——

Published in Australia by: Hay House Australia Pty. Ltd.,
18/36 Ralph St., Alexandria NSW 2015
Phone: 612-9669-4299 • *Fax:* 612-9669-4144
www.hayhouse.com.au

Published in the United Kingdom by: Hay House UK, Ltd.,
The Sixth Floor, Watson House, 54 Baker Street, London W1U 7BU
Phone: +44 (0)20 3927 7290 • *Fax:* +44 (0)20 3927 7291
www.hayhouse.co.uk

Published in India by: Hay House Publishers India,
Muskaan Complex, Plot No. 3, B-2, Vasant Kunj, New Delhi 110 070
Phone: 91-11-4176-1620 • *Fax:* 91-11-4176-1630
www.hayhouse.co.in

——

Access New Knowledge.
Anytime. Anywhere.

Learn and evolve at your own pace
with the world's leading experts.

www.hayhouseU.com